DAYS OUT
With Kids

First published in 1994 by

Two Heads Publishing
12A Franklyn Suite
The Priory
Haywards Heath
West Sussex
RH16 3LB

A catalogue record for this book is available from the
British Library.

Every effort has been made to ensure the accuracy of
information in this book. Details such as opening times
and prices are subject to change and the authors and
publishers cannot accept liability for any errors or
omissions.

ISBN   1-897850-45-X

Illustrations by Sam Toft

Printed & bound by Caldra House Ltd., Hove, Sussex

DAYS OUT
With Kids

30 Great Outings from London
for people with young children

Written and Compiled by Janet Bonthron

**TWO HEADS
PUBLISHING**

Dedicated to Iestyn for his unfailing support,
and to Mair, Jesse, Emma, Jack, Camilla,
Maria, Matthew and Rachel
who helped with the research
in their indefatigable way!

CONTENTS

Look! Look! Look! - exhibitions and things to see

Somewhat Historical - castles and cottages

The Sun Has Got His Hat On - walks and picnics

INTRODUCTION

IF THE CONVERSATION in your house often sounds like that scene in *Jungle Book* where the vultures discuss what they are going to do, then this is the book for you. Welcome to the first edition of 'Days Out with Kids'. Full of ideas, I hope you'll have as much fun using it as we did writing it!

As a mother of two young children I know how important it can be to get out of the house at times - both for the general household mood as well for the childrens' entertainment! Equally, it is often difficult to think of places to go, which are not *too* far, and where children will be well-catered for. Sometimes, after the umpteenth time, the Common or Park does not seem exciting enough, especially with a whole day ahead of you. This book helps you tackle those problems, by offering you my personal selection of great outings to go on with young children.

My aim has been to describe outings which we all enjoyed as a family - with something to interest adults as well as children. A few places are really adult outings, but if you take children they will enjoy the day too, although maybe not in the same way as the adults! I hope that most of them are new to you, and introduce you to some unusual, fun places we have been.

Each of the outings has been personally visited by me and my children often accompanied by our friends and their children. Some are old favourites many times visited. Others are recommendations by friends of places they love. We have noted what facilities are provided for people with young children, for example whether high chairs are available, what the nappy-changing facilities are like, whether it is easy to walk around with a pushchair, and how generally amenable it is for energetic and truculent young children! Many places have excellent child-friendly facilities, but some are less good. However, places haven't been selected purely on the basis of the toilet facilities. Rather I have followed the principle that, if you *know* in advance what is there, you can plan accordingly and enjoy the day. For example, if you know there are limited high chairs, then you might plan to take a blanket and a picnic, or that if nappy-changing facilities are not provided, then you might change the nappy in the car first or whatever. To sum up, each of the places included are in the book because we had a fun day there, and I think that other people with young children could too.

A note on the ages of children covered. My children are both under five, and the trips in the book are ideal for children of that age. I would guess that most of the outings included would also appeal to older children, (many have lots of space, information boards and quizzes etc.) but I will leave it up to you, the reader, to decide whether your own children would enjoy a particular trip.

We visited these places in the winter just as much as summer. It is worth remembering that although many places are lovely in warm weather it is just as possible to have a trip out in the winter and autumn as in spring and summer, and often it will be less crowded.

The facts given for each place have been checked rigorously. However, things do change, and I must stress the need to check details (particularly opening times) before you set out. Telephone numbers are given with each outing to help you do this.

The views and opinions describing each outing are very much my own personal thoughts and reactions. All the visits were done anonymously. If I have been negative in any respect, it is simply based on my experience on the day I visited.

I should love to receive your comments on any places you visit in this book. There is a comments form printed at the back of the book. Equally, let me know of any outings you think could have been included. Please send them to me at Two Heads Publishing - the address is at the front of the book, and I will use any comments I receive in compiling future editions. Thank you.

Janet Bonthron

HOW TO USE THIS BOOK

E ACH SECTION OF the book covers trips which fall into the same broad category of attraction. Outings are described alphabetically within the section. If you know what sort of outing you want to do, then I suggest you just look at the section titles, read the section summaries below, and flick through the entries included in that section. Alternatively, the handy planning guide is a rapid, self-explanatory table for identifying the right trip for you.

Animal Encounters covers trips to farms, zoos and other birds and beasties type places. It is difficult to beat small children and animals as a winning combination, and there are a lot of places around London you can go to which offer it. I have chosen those which I think are distinctive in some way, for example superb handling opportunities for children, wonderful setting, or unusual or imaginatively-displayed animals. Whichever you choose, you can be guaranteed that kids will love it, and will want to return time and again. Try all of them to give yourself some variety!

Up, Down, There and Back has two steam train ride outings, and a steam fairground. Puffs of steam and the smell of smoke in the air are always thrilling for young children and the ones I have included have features which make them particularly accessible. Eat your heart out, Thomas the Tank Engine!

The Great Outdoors is about trips which are all or mostly outdoors in character, in an especially beautiful or quiet setting. Ideal for walks and strolls, with plenty to see for adults whilst the little horrors run around exhausting themselves. Couldn't be better!

Look! Look! Look! features places with exhibitions or displays which young children should particularly enjoy, be they a busy airport runway (Gatwick), a pint-sized town (Bekonscot), or nose-to-nose contact with deep-sea creatures (Brighton Sea Life). These outings offer the chance for children to see something unusual or to experience at close quarters something they may only have seen on television.

The attractions in *Somewhat Historical* all have a theme of things of a bygone age. Your children may not fully appreciate the historical connotations, but will be able to enjoy the setting and exhibits, whilst you can wallow in romantic nostalgia!

Finally, no book on outings would be complete without including a section on eating in the fresh air. There is something about spreading your blanket on the ground and unpacking boxes and plates of picnic food that is just pure summertime, and you can't equal it. The picnic spots I have included in *The Sun Has Got His Hat On* are obviously just a small selection of what is available - most good picnic spots tend to be closely guarded secrets - but these are ones which are favourites of ours. Happy munching! Of course, many of the locations in sections one to five are also excellent picnic spots.

If, on the other hand, you don't mind what sort of attraction you go to, but have other criteria (such as the weather, distance, or means of transport for example) which you need to satisfy, then the best way to use the book is to refer to the map and planning guide given in the next few pages. These should help you to pick a suitable day out. The map indicates the general location of each day out, what else is in the neighbourhood, and the broad route to take.

In the planning guide outings are banded according to travel times. The bands I have used are:

- BAND A ; up to one hours drive
- BAND B ; one to two hours drive
- BAND C ; two or more hours drive

These timings are approximate, and taken from Central South West London (we live in Clapham). The guide also indicates what sort of attraction it is (in line with the section headings given above), the approximate distance in miles form Central South West London, whether opening periods are restricted (i.e. if a place is not open all the year, and/or only on some days of the week), wet weather suitability and accessibility by public transport or otherwise. I have erred on the generous side when deciding on the wet weather suitability - if you don't miss too much by ducking inside somewhere during an occasional shower then I have classified it as 'wet weather suitable'. Unfortunately, public transport is increasingly difficult these days, and you may have to resort to a short, final taxi ride for some outings. I do say in the Fact File given for each attraction if this is the case.

Once you have identified a trip that sounds appealing, refer to the detailed description for further information. Page numbers are given in the Planning Guide. The Fact File which accompanies each entry gives the address and telephone number, travel directions and distances, opening times and prices, and an indication of specific facilities (high chairs, nappy change areas, and eating places). Where appropriate, the Fact File also suggests other nearby attractions.

MAP

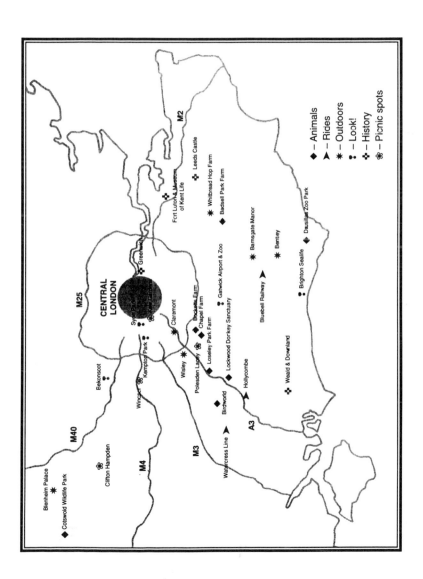

PLANNING GUIDE

OUTING	SECTION	TRAVEL TIME	WET WEATHER	PUBLIC TRANSPORT	OPENING	PAGE
Bocketts Farm Park	Animals	A	Yes	Yes		27
Chapel Farm	Animals	A		Yes	Restricted	30
Loseley Park Farm	Animals	A	Yes		Restricted	42
Hollycombe Steam Collection & Gardens	Rides	A	Yes	Yes	Restricted	49
Claremont Landscape Gardens	Outdoors	A		Yes	Restricted	64
Wisley RHS Gardens	Outdoors	A			Restricted	70
Kempton Park Races	Look!!	A		Yes	Restricted	82
Syon Butterfly House & Park	Look!!	A	Yes	Yes		85
Greenwich - Cutty Sark & Maritime Museum	History	A	Yes	Yes		91
Kew Gardens	Picnics	A		Yes		105
Polesden Lacey	Picnics	A				108
Badsell Park Farm	Animals	B	Yes	Yes	Restricted	21
Birdworld	Animals	B		Yes		24
Drusillas Zoo Park	Animals	B	Yes	Yes		36
Lockwood Donkey Sanctuary	Animals	B		Yes		39
The Bluebell Railway	Rides	B	Yes	Yes	Restricted	45
The Watercress Line	Rides	B	Yes	Yes	Restricted	52
Barnsgate Manor Vineyard	Outdoors	B				55

A - up to one hours drive

B - one to two hours drive

C - two or more hours drive

PLANNING GUIDE

OUTING	SECTION	TRAVEL TIME	WET WEATHER	PUBLIC TRANSPORT	OPENING	PAGE
Bentley Wildfowl & Motor Museum	Outdoors	B			Restricted	58
The Whitbread Hop Farm	Outdoors	B				67
Bekonscot Model Village	Look!!	B		Yes	Restricted	73
Brighton Sea Life Centre	Look!!	B	Yes	Yes		76
Gatwick Airport & Zoo	Look!!	B	Yes	Yes		79
Fort Luton & Kent Life Museum	History	B		Yes	Restricted	88
Leeds Castle	History	B		Yes		95
Weald & Downland Open Air Museum	History	B	Yes	Yes	Restricted	99
Clifton Hampden	Picnics	B				102
Windsor Town & Great Park	Picnics	B		Yes	Restricted	111
Cotswold Wildlife Park	Animals	C				33
Blenheim Palace	Outdoors	C			Restricted	61

A - up to one hours drive

B - one to two hours drive

C - two or more hours drive

ANIMAL ENCOUNTERS - FARMS, ZOOS AND THE LIKE

Badsell Park Farm

THIS IS A well-run small farm that thoughtfully offers several other attractions besides the usual farm animals that young children enjoy so much! It is in an attractive valley in Kent, complete with picture-book oast house, brick farm house, rolling fields and woodland. Although it is possibly more fun in the summer, when you can go fruit picking , the indoor play facilities and farm walks mean that it is also a good trip in spring or autumn.

The farm is set in fruit fields, including strawberries, raspberries, blackberries, gooseberries, Old English apples and pears. In season, you can pick-your-own (or pick-eat-your-own, in our daughter's case!) Be prepared for smeary fingers, and a modest amount of somewhat squashed fruit from your little darlings! Meanwhile, you can get on with the serious business of picking. . . Alternatively you can buy the fruit at the farm shop, but that is less fun.

The Animal Park is home to a number of traditional farm animals, such as goats, ponies, sheep, pigs, cows, as well as geese, chickens and ducks. They live in a grassy enclosed park area, with a small pond and stream running through. The walk around the Animal park is fenced - so there is no danger of falling in the water - but access to the animals is a bit restricted. Pushchairs can easily be pushed round. Some animals are in enclosed sheds, where you can get a close look. When we were there the pig shed had seven five-day-old piglets, as well as other older ones. Pigs are always good value with children because they make such a noise! There is also a small pet area, with lots of different types of rabbits and guinea pigs, though with limited handling.

The walk through the Animal Park ends in a super open play area, with a real *fire engine!* As you can imagine, this has high entertainment potential. The play area also boasts a well-designed wooden fort, complete with climbing ropes and bridge over the

stream. Nearby there is a large, covered sandpit and a tropical butterfly house (only open in summer).

Tractor rides run from just outside the Animal Park entrance (check at the entrance for times), for a 15 minute lurch around the fields in a covered trailer. Buggies can be accommodated. Pony rides are also available, although not on all days. Both tractor and pony rides cost an extra 60p per person (including toddlers). For the more energetic, there are two farm walks available, one about a mile in length, and a shorter one of about half a mile. These both go through fields and ancient woodland, with plenty of wildlife and wildflower interest. They can be muddy after rain and not really suitable for pushchairs.

The cafe is in the oast house, and offers a good range of hot food, sandwiches, cakes and cream teas. There is a very useful gated play corner, with lots of toys for the under-fives. The barn next door has been rebuilt to provide huge new indoor play facilities for up-to-six-year-olds, and birthday parties can be catered for here. There are also picnic areas, including one in a covered barn.

FACT FILE

Address: Badsell Park Farm, Crittenden Road, Matfield,
Tonbridge, Kent

Telephone: 0892 832549

Directions: By car to Sevenoaks and from there take the A21
south towards Tunbridge Wells. Take the Pembury road off the
A21, and the farm is signposted from the roundabout at that
exit. By train from Charing Cross to Paddock Wood, and taxi
from the station (about 2 miles)

Distance from SW London: 44 miles

Travel Time: 1 hour 30 minutes

Opening: From the end of March to November every day, from
10.00am to 5.00pm

Prices: £4.00 adults, £2.50 children, under-2's free.
Farm trail and fruit-picking free

Nappy Changing Facilities: Yes

Restaurant Facilities: Yes

High Chairs: Yes

Nearby: Whitbread Hop Farm (see The Great Outdoors
section)

Birdworld

IF YOU OR your children like birds, Birdworld is a must. Even if you're not bothered about them, it is still a stimulating and unusual day out, amidst pleasant garden surroundings. It is really a zoo for birds, with all sorts of different species - colourful and otherwise - on display and displaying themselves in enclosures and cages. The downside is that, being birds, handling potential by eager little people is limited, if not downright dangerous (ref. the vultures!)! However, there is plenty to see, hear and pick up, indeed at home we are still admiring the display of blue, red and gold feathers we collected from the ground whilst we were there.

The cages and enclosures are well set-out along paths which are easily negotiable with pushchairs. Some enclosures have hedging around them which can be a bit high for toddlers to see over, although there are often holes in the hedge for peering through! In the main, though, most of the birds can readily be seen, especially those in the cages. Some, like the ostrich, are quite friendly (or curious?), which means you can see them at close quarters. At over seven feet tall the ostrich was rather too daunting a prospect for my daughter, who took refuge behind my knees!

There are birds from all over the world. For our children, highlights were the noisy squawking parrots with their bright plumage, the laughing ducks, flamingos and pelicans on the lake, and, of course, Penguin Island. This is home to about 30 penguins, and has a very good underwater viewing enclosure, which lets you see the birds diving and playing underwater. Penguin feeding at 11.30am and 3.30pm is great fun. If you book in advance you can feed them yourself and the £5.00 charge is donated to charity.

Other special features include the seashore walk (terns and oyster catchers), the woodland trail (native birds and trees), and the tropical walk (exotic birds in a heated environment).

The small Jenny Wren farm is also very appealing to youngsters. This has farm animals (goats, pigs, horses, chickens, doves etc.), of which some are roaming around freely, although I'm not

completely sure if that was intentional! On our visit there was much hilarity chasing the rabbits, which tantalisingly hopped a few feet away every time we tried to stroke them.

There is also a safari road train ride, which doesn't run in the winter (50p for a round trip, or 25p for half way, runs weekends from Easter, and weekdays during summer school holidays), and a good children's playground with slides, swings and climbing paraphernalia. This is next to a large picnic area with tables, benches and cafe facilities (pizzas and snacks), as well as toilets with an adequate baby changing bench. There is another cafe and an ice-cream parlour, plus more toilets and a small gift shop at the entrance. There are no high chairs in the cafe.

Adjacent to the Birdworld entrance is Underwater World, which houses a small display of freshwater and marine fish. This, together with the Owl's Nest bookshop, provides a wet weather diversion. Although mud isn't a problem in the main gardens, and some of it is under cover, most of Birdworld is exposed to the elements, and you would need to be suitably waterproofed if it were raining!

FACT FILE

Address: Birdworld, Holt Pound, Farnham, Surrey
GU10 4LD

Telephone: 0420 22140

Directions: A3 to Guildford, and then the A31 (Hogs Back) to Farnham. Signposted from the end of the Hogs Back dual carriageway. Alternatively, signposted from junction 4 of the M3. By train from Waterloo to Aldershot (6 mile bus ride), Farnham (3 mile taxi ride) or Bentley (one and a half mile signposted walk through forest)

Distance from SW London: 40 miles

Travel Time: 1 hour 15 minutes

Opening: 364 days a year from 9.30am. Closing 6.00pm in summer, and 3.45pm in winter

Prices: £3.85 adults, £2.10 children. Under-3's free. Guide book and map £2.00

Nappy Changing Facilities: Yes

Restaurant Facilities: Yes

High Chairs: No

Nearby: Birdworld is set in the Alice Holt forest, which has trails and picnic areas suitable for pushchairs. Near to Frensham Ponds

Bocketts Farm Park

IF YOU THINK you've had enough of squelching around muddy fields, trailing after elusive chickens or rabbits, well, think again, because Bocketts is really very good, being extremely well-equipped to deal with young children (and their hard-pressed carers). Although justifiably popular, it is rarely crowded. You can even have a good time there in the rain (we have done!)

One of the best features of the farm is that the animals are very accessible to children. They are mostly kept in small enclosures in a very large open barn, and within the barn there is a melange of different creatures - when we last visited there were greedy goats, sleepy calves, squealing piglets, sheep, a donkey and an enormous shire horse in residence. Because it is a working farm different animals are inside the barn depending on the time of year: spring is good time for lambs, when you can see them being born or bottle fed. There is a separate area at the back of the barn for smaller animals - rabbits, guinea pigs, ducklings and chicks, all watched over by loud crowing cockerels. All the animals are very friendly and children are encouraged to feed, touch, stroke, and generally admire them. (Bags of feed are on sale at the entrance for 25p a bag). Farm staff are around to talk to, and there are loads of information plaques everywhere, to allow you to bolster your reputation for omniscience. There is plenty of space for pushchairs between the different enclosures.

Outside the barn there is also a lot to see and do. Tame and beautiful red deer (grey in colour) live in a small area next to the barn. You can follow a short walk on a broad path (suitable for pushchairs) round the fields to see horned cows, billy goats and more pigs. On some days there are horse drawn cart, tractor trailer and pony rides (ring to check first - small extra charge). There is also a great playground with old tractors to climb on, an enormous sand pit, and a two storey Wendy house as well as swings, slide and a wooden adventure area. The playground is a good size for the children to have lots of fun, but small enough to let you keep

your eye on the little terrors without having to chase around behind them all the time! On occasions it can be muddy - don't wear your best shoes!

If they tire of the playground and/or it is pouring with rain, the hay bale 'castle' back in the barn is a very popular alternative, with bales to scramble all over and under. Even our crawling babies enjoyed playing with the hay.

When you've had enough you can retire to the spacious and attractive 18th century barn which serves homemade lunches and teas. There is a children's menu, lots of high chairs (mostly with straps), and a small play area with toys. On sunny days nobody seems to mind if some of the toys migrate outside to the large yard. Lunch cost us about £5.00 a head (which included both an adult's and child's portions). The tearoom will cater for birthday parties (£2.50 per child), or you can bring your own party food and use the barn for £10.00. If you want to picnic there are both covered and open areas outside with tables and benches.

The gift shop is well-stocked and sells lots of farm books and toys, as well as the more usual gifts.

FACT FILE

Address: Bocketts Farm Park, Young Street, Fetcham,
Nr Leatherhead, Surrey KT22 9DA

Telephone: 0372 363764

Directions: By car A3 and A24. Signposted from the
Leatherhead roundabout on the A24. By train to Leatherhead or
Fetcham from Waterloo, and short taxi ride

Distance from SW London: 20 miles

Travel Time: 50 minutes

Opening: All year (except 10th-26th January).
10.00am to 6.00pm.

Prices: Adult £2.40, children (3-17 years) £1.75, children
(2 years) £1.00, under-2's free. Reduced rates Monday to
Friday in term times

Nappy Changing Facilities: Yes

Restaurant Facilities: Yes

High Chairs: Yes

Nearby: Polesden Lacey, a NT house and gardens
(see The Sun Has Got His Hat On section)

Chapel Farm

THIS IS A friendly, small farm which is easy to get to, not far from London. It has the usual range of farm animals, which are well displayed for small people, and plenty of opportunities for handling and stroking. For older children, there are lots of informative notices and displays. As it is a working sheep farm, in the summer you may be lucky enough to see sheep shearing , and all through the year there are usually lots of baby animals to admire.

Most of the animals to see are kept in pens and barns surrounding a traditional farm yard, replete with scratching chickens and noisy ducks cavorting in a muddy farm pond. Fencing prevents eager duck-chasers from enjoying splashing in the mud themselves! There are several varieties of pigs, including some of the friendliest we have seen - our 11-month-old was pretty intrigued by his close-up with a Berkshire sow. When we were there Lucy, the proud mother of six piglets, obliged us by prodding them awake with her snout, so we got a good view.

The walk around the farmyard takes about an hour and a half, depending how often you accept the invitation to get in the pens with the animals. Calves, sheep, and goats with huge floppy ears are waiting for you, as well as a Shire horse and Shetland ponies. The lovely Chapel Barn is home to a pair of Barn Owls, but they must have been asleep when we were there. In Flint Barn, which is full of ducklings and chicks, we saw the thrilling spectacle of a chick emerging from its shell. As usual, rabbits and guinea pigs were squealingly popular.

Behind the farm house there is a lovely play area - a good manageable size, with a Land Rover, tractors and huge tractor wheels to play on, and sunny benches so you can rest whilst keeping your eye on your children. Various small farm animals, notably ducks and chickens share the play area.

Don't come to the farm for lunch, unless you bring your own. Refreshment facilities are limited to vending machines with snacks and drinks. However, there are plenty of lovely sites for a picnic,

with benches and tables. You could also shelter in the Honeysuckle Barn for your picnic if you needed to, and the children can also amuse themselves playing Hoopla there.

As well as the farmyard, there is a farm trail through a beautiful wooded valley, with views of nearby Box Hill. This takes about 45 minutes, but could be difficult with a pushchair after wet weather (check in advance). If you don't fancy walking, tractor trailer rides leave half hourly for a half hour trip to the farm boundaries (£1.00 each person). All in all, there is quite enough to keep you and young children amused for a whole day!

FACT FILE

Address: Chapel Farm, West Humble, Dorking, Surrey
RH5 6AY

Telephone: 0306 882865

Directions: By car the farm is off the A24 Dorking road
between Leatherhead and Dorking. Take the right hand turning
off the A24 just beyond the Burford Bridge roundabout,
signposted to Boxhill Station. The farm is about a mile along
this road. By train to Boxhill and Westhumble from Waterloo
(via Clapham Junction). About half a mile walk along the road
(narrow and no pavements) to the farm

Distance from SW London: 20 miles

Travel Time: 45 minutes

Opening: Every day mid February to November
10.00am to 6.00pm

Prices: £1.60 adults and children. Under-2's free

Nappy Changing Facilities: Yes

Restaurant Facilities: No

High Chairs: No

Nearby: Box Hill has lovely walks and space to run about.
The King William pub on the opposite side of the A24 valley to
the farm has good food and gardens for children. Note though
that there is limited room for families inside the pub

Cotswold Wildlife Park

"Tiger, tiger, burning bright. . ."

COME HERE TO SEE wild animals that you can't see on a farm - real tigers, rhinos and zebras to name a few, in 120 acres of gardens and landscaped parkland around a large Gothic style manor house. It is a long way to go - an early start and careful timing to coincide with sleep periods are advised. On the positive side, though, it offers a varied, exciting day out and is just as much fun in winter as summer, so it really is worth the trip.

Despite being terrified of the tiger (well, who wouldn't be?) our children had a wonderful day. On arrival we headed straight for the wildest animals - the leopards, tiger and rhinos. Well-signposted paths radiate out from the car park, so you can easily work out which way to go. Passing what looked like some random tor stones, which suddenly moved towards us, admired the giant tortoises. Despite wanting to ride on them, our daughter was tempted away with promises of more things to come.

After a short walk past a vast, apparently empty field we reached the zebra house, leopard house, and most spectacularly the tigers. Obviously zebras and leopards aren't stupid (it was a cold day) - they were inside, but large glass windows on their houses, with steps up for children, meant we could all get a wonderful view of them. No shivering inside for the tigers - they were prowling around looking highly ferocious, but a close-up sight of those sharp yellow teeth, glinting eyes and huge paws (even safely behind wire netting) proved too much for our daughter and we had to beat a hasty retreat to the relative safety of the Bactrian camels.

Back around the house there are plenty more animals to see - red pandas, monkeys, gibbons and emus are just some of what is on offer. They are all very well displayed, with ditches and viewing platforms enabling you to get a really close up look. To be within six foot of a white rhino is quite an experience and our son was clearly enthralled, although we were not able to persuade him that it wasn't a 'dawg'! There is also a children's farmyard area, with a good display of pot-bellied pigs, angora goats, rabbits, guinea pigs, ducks and poultry. Some of these may be stroked and petted, and they are very accessible for small children to see and appreciate.

The mansion and attached buildings house a number of other attractions, including the reptile and invertebrate houses, and aquarium. Warm, with subdued lighting and suitably impressive slimies and slitheries, these proved very popular, although children have to be lifted to see inside some displays. The bat house, where you can look down on the bats swirling below you, was fascinating. It adjoins the glass animal house, where you can see a myriad of miniature glass animals both on display and being made.

Other areas to visit are the walled garden with otters, meerkats, toucans, hornbills and penguins. The penguins benefit from newly refurbished enclosure, opened in April 1994, and are fed at 11.00am and 4.00pm every day, except Friday. Many more birds, including flamingoes, cranes, swans and ducks can be seen in the lake area. You are not allowed to feed them though. All the paths are easily accessible to pushchairs, including those round the lake, and there are plenty of good, clear information boards and signs.

Behind the house is an adventure playground with slides, swings, climbing equipment and other amusements for children from babyhood to at least eight years old. The helter skelter is quite awe-inspiring and very popular with five-year-olds. I expect the playground could get crowded in busy periods. There is also a narrow gauge railway - trains are always fun - which runs at 20 minute intervals from April to October inclusive and takes you past most of the animals' enclosures (50p charge per person).

The park is very well-served with picnic areas, with a large picnic lawn in front of the house, and picnic tables in several other locations, including the adventure playground. There is a large self-service cafe, with a highly distracting baby dinosaur display (lizards to you and me). High chairs with straps are provided, but were in rather short supply. Half of the seating area is non-smoking. There is also a bar, with seating outside as well as indoors.

During the summer there are many special events, including birds of prey flying demonstrations, morris dancing, and archery tournaments. All in all a great many things are on offer - try it!

FACT FILE

Address: Cotswold Wildlife Park, Burford, Oxon, OX18 4JW

Telephone: 0993 823006

Directions: Take the Oxford exit from the M40. Follow the Oxford ring road north (signposted A40 Cheltenham), and then the A40 to Burford. Signposted from the A40. At Burford turn left off the A40 and the park is about 1 mile down on the right

Distance from SW London: 80 miles

Travel Time: 2 hours

Opening: 10.00am to 6.00pm or dusk, whichever earlier. Open every day except Christmas Day

Prices: £4.20 adults, £2.70 children over 4. Under-4's free

Nappy Changing Facilities: Yes

Restaurant Facilities: Yes

High Chairs: Yes, limited

Nearby: Oxford, Blenheim Palace (see The Great Outdoors section), Cogges Farm Museum at Witney (0993 772602)

Drusillas Zoo Park

THE ANIMALS AT Drusillas have all been selected for their appeal to young children. The zoo lives up well to its own description as 'the best small zoo in the country', both in terms of the child-sized animals there and the compact, manageable area to walk around. However, don't be mistaken, there is certainly a lot to see - we spent a full day there, amid shrieks of pleasure, and had the added benefit of very sleepy children on the way home! It was very popular when we went though, (during the school holidays) and correspondingly very hectic.

The zoo is imaginatively laid-out, with a secession of different themed areas - evolution, farm animals, climbing animals and monkeys, Australian outback, Beaver country, Wind in the Willows, to name a few. Participation and understanding of the animals are encouraged with lots of brain teasers, quizzes and physical 'tests'. For example, the children are invited to try hanging like a monkey on poles, milking a very life-like cow, or running as fast as a llama on all-fours. All the animals may be viewed easily by toddlers, and there is plenty of space for them to run around, and to manoeuvre a buggy. You can even crawl into one of the enclosures through a tunnel and pop up inside a large dome for real eye-ball to eye-ball contact with a troop of meerkats (small furry rodents, long necks). The displays are great fun and really brought the zoo to life. Quite a lot of parent interaction is called for though, so if you are feeling particularly jaded - be warned!

Events such as feeding times, when staff get in the cages and 'play' with some animals, and special attractions, for example, the baby animals, are well worth a look. The staff are easily recognisable in red 'Drusillas' tee-shirts and trousers: those we spoke to were very friendly and helpful. During the school holidays animal handling sessions (rabbits and guinea pigs) are held between 11.45am to 12.45pm and 2.00pm to 3.00pm.

Other attractions include four play areas: a toddler tumble, an under-six-year-old tumble room, a general play area with an SAS-

looking style apparatus, and an indoor playbarn - useful on a rainy day. These are busy during the school holidays, but highly tempting for children, containing a customised tractor, fire engine and wooden houses to play in and on. There are two trains in operation offering trips around the park, but queuing time to get on a train was about 20 minutes when we were there.

There is a choice of several places to eat and an area for you to enjoy your own picnics. The Inn at the Zoo is open at all times and has hot and cold lunches. Toucans Restaurant is open weekends and school holidays during the week, with lots of high chairs, friendly and helpful service, and charges approximately £2.00 to £3.00 for a child's main course. The Inn at the Zoo offers pub food and teas, and has a restful and quiet garden, with live music and plenty of space for children to tire themselves out running around.

Several shops are dotted about - including a gift shop, toy shop, fudge factory, and wacky workshop. About a third of the zoo is under cover, so it would be possible to go in wet weather.

FACT FILE

Address: Drusillas Park, Alfriston, East Sussex BN26 5QS

Telephone: 0323 870234

Directions: By car take the M23/A23, and then the A27 to Lewes. Follow the A27 on towards Polegate, and Drusillas is signposted off at the Wilmington roundabout. By train to Polegate from Victoria or Clapham Junction, with a good taxi service from the station (3 miles)

Distance from SW London: 54 miles

Travel Time: 1 hour 30 minutes

Opening: Daily throughout the year, except Christmas and Boxing Days. Open from 10.00am to 5.00pm in the summer (last admission), and until 4.00pm in the winter

Prices: Adults £4.95, children over 3, £4.35

Nappy Changing Facilities: Yes

Restaurant Facilities: Yes

High Chairs: Yes

Nearby: Brighton Sea Life Centre (see the Look! Look! Look! section). The Alfriston Heritage Centre (open Easter to the end of October) has a blacksmith's museum, historical exhibition and lovely walks (0323 870303)

Lockwood Donkey Sanctuary

TRY A VISIT here if you are feeling unloved. With a bucket of scrubbed carrots on your arm (available at the shop for £1.00) the 160 donkeys will go out of their way to make you feel welcome, and you will definitely be very popular! Young children seem to be untiringly thrilled by close encounters with animals, and Lockwood gives plenty of opportunity to get to know the donkeys, who all are very gentle and friendly. So friendly, in fact, that my daughter hardly murmured when she was nudged into a puddle by an over-enthusiastic beast.

Located in a beautiful wooded part of Surrey, the Sanctuary is a home for several other sorts of animals, besides donkeys, cared for in a peaceful, rural environment. (Peaceful, that is, apart from the squeals of delight from young visitors as their carrots are efficiently removed from them). There are goats, horses (also keen on carrots), pigs, dogs, a wallaby, a deer and at least one llama. Plus the usual squawking geese, ducks, and chickens that you come to expect on these days out. All the animals can be visited in stables and fields which surround a large traditional farmyard, complete with authentic steaming manure! You are free to wander around the farmyard, and we had no trouble taking a buggy everywhere.

There is an 'adopt a donkey scheme' which costs £1.00 for children, £2.00 for adults, and gives you a certificate and regular newsletters.

Facilities are somewhat limited. There are some picnic tables and rudimentary toilets, and the shop sells some drinks (as well as second-hand books and clothes, and carrots). During the summer there are special event days when more is on offer - stalls, teas and animal parades. Apart from these days, it is probably a good idea to combine a visit to Lockwood with another attraction, for example Wisley Gardens (see The Great Outdoors section), or see the suggestions in the Fact File.

FACT FILE

Address: Lockwood Donkey Sanctuary, Farm Cottage, Hatch lane, Sandhills, Wormley, Near Godalming, Surrey

Telephone: 0428 682409

Directions: By car, take the Haselmere turn off the A3, and follow the A283 Petworth road, before turning right to Sandhills at Wormley. The Sanctuary is three quarters of a mile from the A283 turnoff, signposted down a rough road on the left. By train to Witley station, and a 10 minute walk along a footpath (ask at the station for directions)

Distance from SW London: 38 miles

Travel Time: 1 hour

Opening: All year - 8.30am to 5.30pm or dusk

Prices: Free, donations welcome

Nappy Changing Facilities: No

Restaurant Facilities: No

High Chairs: No

Nearby: Walks on Sandhills Common (National Trust). Painshill Park is a beautiful park and gardens near Cobham, open Sundays from April to October (0932 868113). The White Hart pub at Whiteley has pub meals and a children's playground. Guildford's Spectrum Leisure centre has a great swimming pool and creche (0483 444777)

Loseley Park Farm

L OSELEY PARK IS a beautiful Elizabethan house set in a 1,400 acre estate, consisting of gardens, woodland, and of course, pasture for the famous Loseley Dairy herd. No need to remind ice cream connoisseurs that the renowned Loseley Dairy products are made here! Although you can visit the splendid house (45 minute guided tours, pushchairs not admitted), the main attraction for those with youngsters in tow is the chance to be shown around a working dairy farm. The grounds are also fabulous, with great walking potential, and you are able to picnic in some lovely spots. At the edge of the car park there is a covered open barn with benches and tables, which is ideal for picnics, especially in damp weather.

The farm tours run in the afternoons (from about 12 noon), and start with a tractor trailer ride. This is covered and large enough to take a pushchair complete with sleeping baby! The ride was very popular with our toddlers, bumping and jolting us slowly down from in front of the house to Orange Court Farm. On the way you pass some of the 165 Jersey cows belonging to the estate: beautiful, elegant beasts with liquid brown eyes.

At the farm, there is plenty of opportunity to get to know the herd better. You can visit the bulls with rings in their noses (Jerseys are reputedly the fiercest bulls around!), stroke some of the many calves, and go into the milking shed. If you time your trip right (about 3.30pm) you can actually watch the cows being milked, eight at a time. Other animals on the farm include pigs, rare poultry, and 43 different varieties of sheep. Our helpful guide willingly delved into the chicken run to rescue black and white spotted guinea fowl feathers for the children to have, and handed out handfuls of soft sheep's wool to be taken home. The tour lasts just over an hour, and returns you, on the trailer again, back in front of the house. Although the farm visit was a bit muddy (wellies recommended), it is all negotiable with pushchairs.

Have tea in the tithe barn to the right of the house. This serves

reasonably-priced wholefood cakes, snacks, hot food and drinks, is lovely and large, and has a wooden floor ideal for crawling children. There is a limited number of high chairs. The shop sells Loseley products (don't forget to bring a cool bag!), as well as home-baked bread. There is a nappy changing area in the spacious Ladies toilets at the back.

The newly-opened Nature trail is a one mile walk through the woods, lovely at all times, but especially in May, when the ground is covered with bluebells. It is probably too rough for pushchairs though. Finally, the walled gardens at the side of the house are also worth a visit. The moat walk there is lovely, but toddlers will need watching because of the open water in the moat. The rambling old mulberry tree is particularly noteworthy in late summer when it is covered with delicious, squashy berries.

FACT FILE

Address: Loseley House, Compton, Nr Guildford, Surrey

Telephone: 0483 505501/304440

Directions: Signposted off the A3, just beyond Guildford

Distance from SW London: 30 miles

Travel Time: 45 minutes

Opening: May to September. Wednesdays to Sundays 2.00pm to5.00pm. Grounds open from 11.00am. Restaurant and shop 11.00am to 5.00pm. House closed on Sundays

Prices: Grounds and farm trailer ride £4.00 adults, £2.00 children over three; house, grounds and trailor ride combined £5.40 adults, £3.15 children. Under-3's free

Nappy Changing Facilities: Yes

Restaurant Facilities: Yes

High Chairs: Yes (limited numbers)

Nearby: Lockwood Donkey Sanctuary (see previous outing). Spectrum Leisure Centre at Guildford with swimming pool and creche

UP, DOWN, THERE AND BACK
- TRAINS AND FAIRS

The Bluebell Railway

"The Engineer said he rang the bell
And she blew, Whoo-oo-oo!"

THERE WILL BE enough bells ringing, steam hissing and smoke blowing down on the Bluebell Line to satisfy even the most ardent Thomas the Tank Engine enthusiast. For older train spotters, a trip on the Bluebell railway really conjures up the mythical Golden Age of steam - a time when to travel by train was an excitement and a pleasure in its own right, and trains ran on time! (Ponder on this next time you squash onto the 7.49). Be warned though, it can be very busy at peak weekends (avoid Mothers Day!). However, it does run all year, so it is a good trip to do in the winter, and is a good option in wet weather.

It consists of a re-claimed stretch of railway line running about four miles north from Sheffield Park Station (near Haywards Heath) towards East Grinstead. Volunteers have lovingly amassed a wonderful collection of old steam trains and station memorabilia, and you can take rides up and down the line in old Southern Region carriages pulled by restored steam trains.

We started the day at Sheffield Park station, where there is a large car park. You can also start at Horsted Keynes, the next station on the line. At Sheffield Park a short walk takes you to the station Booking Office and waiting room, where coal fires laid during the winter add to the nostalgia created by the unmistakeable cokey smell of steam trains which is all around. The station is a bustling flurry of people and announcements as the trains arrive and depart. Be prepared to mingle with an incongruous mix of hordes of delighted children and and anoraked train-spotters.

There is plenty to see at the station, but we decided to get straight

on a train and were treated to a dose of instant nostalgia. Remember
that smoky smell of brown velveteen seats, sliding windows you
can just manage to peep out of, and mirrors in the carriages where
you could check your first attempts at make-up? Children will
love the thrill of doors slamming, whistles blowing and the guard
waving his green flag, before the train chugs slowly along through
beautiful Sussex countryside. Watch out for sheep and horses in
the adjoining fields.

The trip to Horsted Keynes station takes about 15 minutes. The
station is an authentic re-creation of the bygone heyday of the
railways, complete with a coffin carrier, and mounds of leather-
bound suitcases and trunks. You can get off there for a look round,
good views of the comings and goings of trains and carriages, or
for walks in the woods (good for bluebells in May). Alternatively
you can go on to New Combe Bridge, where the engine is swapped
to the other end of the train, before returning. From April 1994
you can go further to the newly restored and re-opened Kingscote
station (not yet open when we visited).

Back at Sheffield Park Station, there is plenty to amuse young children. Stroll over the iron footbridge and look down on the engines busying backwards and forwards, or stopping to be refilled with water from an enormous water pipe. On the opposite platform there is a small museum of train and station memorabilia, and a model railway of Horsted Keynes in the 1920's (not operational in January, February and March). Take a peep into the gleaming signals box with labelled handles, and walk right alongside the locomotives, watching the fires being stoked and the pistons throbbing, before, with smoke pouring, they slowly pull out of the station.

At the rear of the station is the engine workshop, where you can walk between the rails right next to the collection of huge locomotives and carriages. Impressive sounding banging and scrapings were coming from the renovation section when we were there. It all added to the atmosphere - particularly for our little boy!

Restaurant and cafe facilities are good. At Sheffield Park station you have the choice of a reproduction Victorian pub, serving meals and with a full bar (real ales served), or the Puffers self service cafe upstairs, which has hot and cold meals, snacks, and drinks. We ate lunch there for just over £10 (two adults and two toddlers). There were only two high chairs though. At Horsted Keynes there is an original 1882 station buffet, again with a full bar service. If you feel like lashing out, Pullman carriages on Sunday trains offer lunches or cream teas (no high chairs on trains).

Alternatively, there are some picnic spots near the stations and picnic tables next to the platforms at all the stations. There is a small platform shop at Sheffield Park which sells a host of train items - toys, books, videos, crockery etc., as well as basics such as films, guide books and post cards.

Trains run at intervals of between 45 minutes to an hour and a half, depending on the time of year and day, so it is worth checking times in advance if you do not want to hang about too much. They start from mid-morning and run through to tea-time. A round trip takes about an hour to an hour and a quarter.

FACT FILE

Address: The Bluebell Railway, Sheffield Park Station,
Nr Uckfield, East Sussex TN22 3QL

Telephone: 0825 723777 (bookings and enquiries)
0825 722370 (24 hour information)

Directions: By car take the M23 and A23, and leave at the
junction with the A272 at Bolney. Follow the brown Bluebell
railway signs from there - it is about a 20 minutes drive from
the A23. Take care following the signs through Haywards
Heath, they are a bit elusive. Train to Haywards Heath, with
bus connections to Sheffield Park running most Saturdays,
some Sundays and some weekdays through the summer
(ring the train information number above for details)

Distance from SW London: 45 miles

Travel Time: 1 hour 30 minutes

Opening: Weekends throughout the year. Weekdays from the
beginning of May to the end of September, plus during Easter
week, last week in October, and Christmas week. Ring in
advance to check timetable

Prices: Admission and return trip, adult £7.00, children 3 to 14
years old £3.50, family (2 adults, 3 children) £19.00. Station
only £2.00 adult, £1.00 child

Nappy Changing Facilities: Yes, table in Ladies toilet at
Sheffield Park

Restaurant Facilities: Yes

High Chairs: Yes, limited, but with straps

Nearby: Sheffield Park Gardens are about a mile further down
the road. Beautiful National Trust gardens with gravelled paths
for pushchairs. Not open in the winter

Hollycombe Steam Collection and Gardens

"Mind You Hold On Tight!"

IT WAS TEEMING with rain, and we only had one pair of wellies between four of us. With drips running down our necks we resolutely struck out towards the fairground. Groups of overall-clad enthusiasts with coal-smeared hands and smutty faces were busy around several huge gleaming engines. Furnaces roared, smoke billowed, and pistons trembled. Suddenly with a 'Tralalala,Bombom,Bombom,Boom-Babaa!' a fairground organ burst into life. We were at the funfair!

Hollycombe is a brilliant day out. Despite the rain we had a marvellous time. There is lots to do and to chose from. First there is the fairground, with about eight different, traditional rides: galloping horses carousel, big wheel, razzle dazzle tilt wheel, and steam yachts, to name a few. Our toddler went on some of these, but really loved the juvenile rides (strict notices informed us that adults are not permitted on these!), where she was spoiled for choice on the roundabout between the fire engine with ladder and bell, double decker bus or airplane (she 'compromised' by having a go on all three). Luckily, the entry ticket enables you to have unlimited numbers of rides!

When you want a change from the fairground, there are no less than three different train rides to pick from. The longest is a mile and a half ride on a narrow gauge railway, pulled by the locomotive 'Jerry'. This passes through woodland, along a ridge with wonderful views of the South Downs, and even through a tunnel. Then there is a miniature railway, with its own station and clock tower, and finally, the huge 'Commander B' locomotive (lots of puff and whistles), which pulls two carriages along a short standard gauge railway. All these rides offer protection from the rain in covered carriages.

There is also a steam tractor and trailer which take you down to

the farm, where you can see a plough and working steam farm equipment, as well as some farm animals. For real steam fans there are other engines too.

Finally, there are the gardens. Mostly woodland, with great views, and wonderful azaleas and daffodils in the Spring, you can go for a lovely walk whilst your children explore. Only limited access with pushchairs though!

Although the steam equipment doesn't get going until 2.00pm, you can go in earlier to walk in the gardens or have something to eat in the covered cafe. This offers basic refreshments such as drinks, sandwiches, pasties etc. No high chairs though. There are plenty of good picnic spots. The gift shop sells souvenirs, toys, postcards, and general train items. Parents of Thomas the Tank engine fans beware!

Hollycombe is run by about 40 volunteers and those we met were unfailingly helpful, very enthusiastic, and willing to answer questions. They run several events through the year, such as craft fairs and model days, as well as Santa Specials at Christmas (fewer steam rides are available then and you need to book in advance).

FACT FILE

Address: Hollycombe Steam Collection & Gardens, Iron Hill, Liphook, Hampshire GU30 7LP

Telephone: 0428 724900 (open days), 0420 474740 (all year)

Directions: By car use the A3 from London. Signposted and about 2 miles drive from A3, through Liphook village. By train from Waterloo or Clapham Junction to Liphook. Although Hollycombe is only about 1 mile from Liphook Station, it is an uphill walk along a lane with no footpath - not recommended with young children, so you would probably have to get a taxi from the station

Distance from SW London: 45 miles

Travel Time: 1 hour

Opening: Sundays and Bank Holidays from Easter until mid October. Daily during much of the summer holidays. From about 1.00pm to 6.00pm. Rides from 2.00pm

Prices: £4.50 adults, £3.50 children (under 2's free), for unlimited rides. Family ticket (2 adults, and 2 children £14.00)

Nappy ChangingFacilities: No

Restaurant Facilities: Cafe

High Chairs: No

Nearby: Dene Farm, a small farm with many animals for handling

The Watercress Line

THE STATION MASTER 'toot-toots' his whistle, the guard smartly waves a green flag, and with gasp of steam and a belching cloud of billowing white smoke the huge locomotive heaves us out of the station. We're off!

If your children like the noise, bustle and excitement of real steam trains, then the Watercress Line is a must. It is a restored 10 mile stretch of railway running between Alton and Alresford in a beautiful rural part of Hampshire. There are currently three locomotives working - two steam, and one diesel -which are used to pull the carriages, as well as seven others in various stages of restoration. The four stations on the line, Alton, Medstead and Four Marks, Ropley, and Alresford, are all preserved and authentically recreate different periods in the railway's history, from the Twenties, to the late Fifties, with staff in appropriate uniforms, and period decoration and equipment. Our toddler loved it, especially being able to go inside the engine cab, and see all the shining knobs and dials!

For a good day out, start at Alton rail station (see how to get there in the fact file), and catch the train to Alresford in the morning. Rather incongruously, the platforms adjoin the commuter station. The journey takes about half an hour, with the train travelling through some lovely countryside as well as deep wooded cuttings. Alresford, when you get there, is a charming small town, with a lovely Georgian High Street, and several shops including antique and secondhand books (some open on Sundays). Have lunch outside at the Swan Hotel on the corner, or take a secret walk back to the station via the churchyard, catching a train back to Ropley, where you can picnic above the railway line, and watch the trains go by (marquee provided for wet weather). It is worth spending some time at Ropley in the afternoon, to see the engine shed with locomotives in the process of being restored - lots of grimy excitement here! You can also stop at the other stations: from Four Marks station there are two signposted woodland walks which are about a mile long. Great picnic potential here, but limited access with pushchairs.

If you fancy a cream tea take the Countryman Special back to Alton (you need to book this in advance). If you have time, you can have an enjoyable walk round Alton (pick up a walk description leaflet at the station), including feeding the ducks on Kings Pond, five minutes walk from the station.

The Watercress line runs on most Sundays of the year, Saturdays too from May to the end of October, and during the week at Easter and the summer months. Check the timetable in advance, as there are several different ones in operation. There are also lots of special events, such as a Teddy Bears Day, Thomas the Tank Engine weekends, Morris Day (Morris men and cars!), and Santa Specials at Christmas.

The Line is run by volunteers, and everyone is very enthusiastic and helpful. Buffet facilities are on most trains and at the station restaurant in Alresford, as well as snacks at the station shops at Alton and Ropley. The shops sell the usual souvenirs and postcards. The steps over the railway line at Alton were a bit awkward with a pushchair, and the trains themselves a bit narrow (single pushchairs okay, but double buggies beware!).

FACT FILE

Address: The Watercress Line, Alresford Station, Hampshire SO24 9JG

Telephone: 0962 733810/734200 Timetable: 0962 734866

Directions: By car take the A3 and A31 to Alton. Parking facilities at Alton and Alresford (pay and display). By train there is a regular train service from Waterloo (stops at Clapham Junction and Wimbledon)

Distance from SW London: 45 miles

Travel Time: 1 hour 30 minutes

Opening: Sundays throughout the year, Saturdays from April to end October. Weekdays at Easter, and during the summer. Trains every 45 minutes to 1 hour 30 minutes depending on season (check timetable in advance)

Prices: Adults £6.50, children 5 to 15 years old £4.50. Under -5's free, except for Special Events, when 2 to 4 year-olds pay £2.50

Nappy Changing Facilities: In Ladies toilet at Alresford

Restaurant Facilities: Buffet facilities and snacks

High Chairs: No

Nearby: Alton and Alresford are both pleasant towns to walk around. The Devil's Punchbowl at Hindhead (20 miles away) is a great picnic and walks area

THE GREAT OUTDOORS - GARDENS AND ATTRACTIONS

Barnsgate Manor Vineyard

B ARNSGATE IS A slightly different day out - a visit which is mainly of interest for adults, although within a safe environment for children too. We treated ourselves to a very peaceful and relaxing day there.

The vineyard was set up in the early 1970's and makes English white wine and sparkling wine from 12 acres of vines. It is set in a lovely sunny bowl of hills in the Weald, overlooking the South Downs, and has stunning views south from the restaurant terrace. The wine struck us (on the basis of no great expertise) as eminently drinkable, if not ecstatically memorable.

The main interest, apart from wine tasting, is the vineyard walk. This takes approximately three quarters of an hour, and takes you round all the main areas of the vineyard. Apart from the vines set out in perfect rows, there are animals to see: llamas, donkeys and Black Wensleydale sheep. These are very friendly, and came to have their noses rubbed and their ears scratched. The walk is well-marked, and has an accompanying descriptive leaflet and map. It is possible to do it with a pushchair (we did).

There is a small shop with lots of wine and other gifts. This is next to the function rooms: our little girl was delighted to see a real bride arriving for her reception. This, however, may be difficult to arrange for your visit - Saturday afternoons in the summer are probably the best bet! There is also a museum illustrating traditional methods of winemaking.

For a good day out come to the vineyard in the morning, do the walk, and then have lunch on the terrace. The tearoom is open for morning coffee, lunches, afternoon and cream teas, whilst the restaurant serves lunch from about 12noon to 2.00pm. A few high chairs are available. There is a lovely grassy area in front of the terrace where children can enjoy running about. You could then

visit the shop and museum, and/or fit in another local attraction in the afternoon before returning home. (See Fact File for suggestions). However, you could always stay and have tea too!

FACT FILE

Address: Barnsgate Manor, Herons Ghyll, Nr Uckfield, East Sussex TN22 4DB

Telephone: 0825 713366

Directions: M25 and then M23 East Grinstead exit. Pick up the A22 at East Grinstead and follow it in the direction of Eastbourne. Before Nutley turn left off the A22 and head for Poundgate. When you get to the A26 turn right and follow signs. The vineyard is off the A26, between Crowborough and Uckfield

Distance from SW London: 50 miles

Travel Time: 1 hour 30 minutes

Opening: From 10.00am to dusk, every day of the year

Prices: Free admission to Vineyard. Vineyard Walk £1.50 adults, 75p for children, and free for under-2's

Nappy Changing Facilities: No

Restaurant Facilities: Yes

High Chairs: Yes

Nearby: Lovely walks in the Ashdown Forest, with plenty of car parking space. Hever Castle near Edenbridge (between East Grinstead and Sevenoaks) is open from March to November and has glorious gardens

Bentley Wildfowl and Motor Museum

"There once was an ugly duckling. . ."

W ITH ITS RATHER incongruous combination of vintage cars and waterfowl, Bentley is sure to appeal to most families! Set in an elegant country estate deep in the Sussex countryside it offers plenty for a good day out.

Depending on the weather, it is probably best to start with the birds. This gives you the chance to get rid of the bags of birdfood that your children will have persuaded you to buy at the entrance for 25p a bag. The birds are all 'housed' (or should it be 'nested'?) in a large series of enclosures, with wide pushchair-friendly paths. Some paths can be slightly muddy in places - especially after periods of wet weather. There is a lot of open water, and although most of it is fenced, you will need to be a bit careful with toddlers. There is a choice of three routes around the enclosures - taking 30, 45 or 60 minutes respectively. Each route leads you through part of the collection - there are over 1000 swans, geese and ducks which can be readily seen and appreciated. Collect an identification chart at the entrance and children will love spotting all the different varieties. Designed with close contact between birds and visitors in mind, there are plenty of opportunities for both adults and children to see the birds at close quarters - especially if you have food for them.

The motor museum should appeal to all car-freaks, large and small. The collection is very impressive. It is under cover and ranges from a 1960's bubble car (when did you last see one of those?), through gleaming Ferrari and Aston Martin sports numbers, to dinky-toy-like Vintage cars and bicycles. Unsurprisingly, children are not allowed to climb on the cars - well would you trust your precious antiques? - nevertheless it is a bit of a shame.

Outside again, the grounds have several further attractions. There is a woodland walk which takes about half an hour, and is resplendent in spring and summer with daffodils and bluebells.

This may be passable in the summer with a pushchair, but when we went it was too muddy. A miniature steam train offers a short ride for 40p per person (under-threes free) on all open Sundays and on Wednesdays too in the summer school holidays. This is being extended and in summer 1995 will take you through the woodland. At the moment it just does a 600m circuit (though you do go round three times!). It runs about every five or ten minutes. There is also a nice adventure playground - not specifically designed for under-fives, but of course they loved it anyway.

Food and drinks are available in the small, pleasant tea-room. Should you wish to sit outside there are also tables in the courtyard. The tea-room has a limited, but adequate, menu of baked potatoes, sandwiches, pasties and ... baked potatoes, as well as teas and cakes. There is only one high chair. However, the extensive grassy grounds offer plenty of potential picnic spots.

Next to the tea-room there is a barn used as a small animal enclosure with pigs (complete with piglets when we visited), sheep, rabbits and a chinchilla. The chinchilla kept himself to himself, but the other occupants provided yet another happy diversion.

FACT FILE

Address: Bentley Wildfowl and Motor Museum, Halland, East Sussex BN8 5AF

Telephone: 0825 840573

Directions: From the M25 take the A22 south to East Grinstead and on in the direction of Eastbourne. Beyond Uckfield look for a brown sign off the A22, and after about 2 or 3 miles follow white signs to Bentley

Distance from SW London: 50 miles

Travel Time: 1 hour 30 minutes

Opening: Daily from late March to the end of October 10.30am to 4.30pm. Weekends only in November, February and first half of March. Closed the rest of the year

Prices: Adults £3.60, children £2.00, under-4's free. Family ticket (2 adults and up to 4 children) £9.95. Reduced rates during the winter

Nappy Changing Facilities: Yes

Restaurant Facilities: Yes

High Chairs: Yes (one)

Nearby: Barkham Manor Vineyard on the A272 between Haywards Heath and Uckfield offers wine tasting, vineyard trail, picnic site and tours of winery (0825 722103). For more vintage cars you could visit the Filching Manor Motor Museum, about 15 miles further on at Jevington just off the A22 near Eastbourne (0323 487838)

Blenheim Palace

M AKE THE TREK to Blenheim Palace when everyone is in the mood for a real day out. Despite being a long journey, there are several attractions there to tempt you, and it is situated in beautiful Capability Brown parkland with a lake. For children the main interest is in the Pleasure Garden, where there are a walled games area, butterfly house, adventure playground and gardens, but there is also plenty of open parkland with great walks.

The Pleasure Garden is a ten minutes walk behind the Palace itself. If you don't fancy the walk, there is a small single gauge railway that gets there in a few minutes, running from near the car park by the Palace. Trains run from 11.00am to 5.30pm, departing every half an hour. If you are aiming to go down at lunch time get to the station early, as a long queue forms at busy times. Similarly, the last trains back in the evening often fill up.

The highlights of the Pleasure Garden are within the walled games area. To enter this is £1.00 per adult, and you need to negotiate a tall, narrow turnstile with no separate pushchair entrance. Folding buggies can probably be passed over the top, but less portable pushchairs would need to be left at the entrance.

Inside the walled area is a large grassy play space, bisected by several paths and with a central fenced-off pond. The Marlborough Maze lies to the left, and is great fun. We weren't deterred by the notices saying buggies aren't permitted in the maze (as it contains two bridges with steps - these can easily be negotiated by experienced buggy users!) We solved the maze in about 20 minutes, with a great deal of cheating on the part of certain small people, who had a tendency to wriggle through gaps in the hedges!

Our children particularly enjoyed running around on the large plastic puzzle path, and hi-jacking the oversized chess men and horses from the adjacent chess set. Chasing balls from the putting green was also very popular - although not with the people trying to play! Also, don't miss the model village. Although only one street long, it is crammed with tiny windows and courtyards for peering in. There is also a bouncy castle for two-to-five-year-olds, 50p per child. Outside the walled garden, the butterfly house is well worth a visit, although a bit difficult to negotiate with buggies. There are lots of brightly coloured flowers and butterflies.

The adventure playground is impressive, with a separate under-fives area. Needless to say, few toddlers are satisfied with staying in their 'ghetto', and they tend to mingle with the older children on the rest of the equipment. This can be somewhat hair-raising!

You could easily spend a whole morning or afternoon at the Pleasure Gardens. However, near the Palace are lovely views and easy walks on broad grassy paths - ideal for toddlers and pushchairs. There are two marked circuits - the Fisheries Cottage walk takes about half an hour, and incorporates the cottage with its hens, wildfowl, and teeming trout in the lake inlet, whilst the other walk is longer (about an hour) and gives marvellous views of the park and Palace. Look out for sheep and lambs in the Spring.

On the lake you can hire rowing boats for between £2.00 and £5.00 per hour, depending on the size of boat. Boats are not hired out in windy weather.

The Palace itself is magnificent, with Churchill memorabilia and a host of grand rooms with paintings and tapestries. Water terraces, and a formal Italian Garden complete the picture of opulence. Tours leave every ten minutes, and last an hour. Pushchairs are admitted.

Eating facilities are good, with a spacious cafe in the Pleasure Gardens serving sandwiches, hot snacks, drinks and cakes. It has a terrace and lawn outside with benches and tables. A few high chairs are available. By the Palace there are two shops - one selling soft drinks and confectionery, and the other gifts and books. However, on a sunny day you could not do better than take a picnic into the park and admire the grandeur of the site whilst munching!

FACT FILE

Address: Blenheim Palace, Woodstock, Oxon

Telephone: 0993 811325 or 0993 811091 weekdays

Directions: By car take the M40 beyond Oxford, and then follow the signs

Distance from SW London: 70 miles

Travel Time: 2 hours

Opening: Pleasure Garden and Palace from March to October every day from 10.30am to 4.45pm.
The park is open all year

Prices: All-inclusive ticket £6.00 adults, £3.30 children from 5 years old. Under-5's free. Park-only, £3.80 per car including all occupants

Nappy Changing Facilities: No

Restaurant Facilities: Yes

High Chairs: Yes

Nearby: Oxford, with its parks and river walks, is always a pleasant place to visit.

Claremont Landscape Gardens

DESIGNED AND ESTABLISHED in the Eighteenth century, and modified by Capability Brown, these gardens have recently been restored by the National Trust to form a peaceful and spacious area to stroll around within easy reach of London. For people with young children they offer an opportunity to wander in apparently natural surroundings of open countryside, but with paths for pushchairs and availability of other essential facilities (food, drink, loos, drink, loos and food!). Be warned, however, there is a large unfenced area of open water in the middle of the gardens, so you will need to keep an eye on toddlers.

The car park and entrance kiosk are at the bottom of the gardens, near to the lake. You can follow the path round the lake, stopping to admire the many different kinds of wildfowl - Aylesbury, Mandarin, and Mallard ducks, black swans, and grebes, to name a few. As ever, the ducks are very amenable to being fed - a reliable toddler-diverting pastime - so bring some bread with you. The lake is also teeming with huge, glossy carp which glide just below the surface. They will actually come up and break the surface if you feed them (not recommended for those who didn't enjoy 'Jaws'!).

A third of the way round the lake is a precarious-looking pile of rocks, otherwise known as the grotto. This is great for those who like dripping, moss-infested caves and crannies. If you don't, move on quickly and you will come round to the other side of the lake, and have a good view of the island with its pavilion house (no access unfortunately), and the Ha-Ha (a grassy ditch to you and me). All around are huge, magnificent trees, and you can pick up a guide to them at the entrance kiosk, so that young children can have fun identifying them as you go round. Some trees date from as far back as the seventeenth and eighteenth centuries.

Once you are on the other side of the lake, the gardens open out more and there are plenty of wide, grassy areas, ideal for resting, having a picnic, or general running around. The gardens continue

up a hill behind the lake, and you can walk up through a camellia terrace, and along a lawned bowling green, before stopping to admire the panorama from the amphitheatre at the top of the gardens. Return down to the lake via a path at the side of the amphitheatre.

The shop and cafe are small and clean, with two high chairs. There are some benches and tables outside too. The cafe sells hot meals from 12.00pm to 2.00pm, and teas, cakes, and drinks the rest of the time. The shop sells National Trust gifts, books and presents.

FACT FILE

Address: Claremont Landscape Gardens, Portsmouth Road, Esher, Surrey KT109JG

Telephone: 0372 469421

Directions: By car, take the A3, and exit at the Esher turnoff. Go through Esher town centre, and follow signs to the gardens, which are located on the A307, just south of Esher. By train to Esher, and about a 2 mile taxi ride from the station

Distance from SW London: 15 miles

Travel Time: 30 minutes

Opening: All year, from 10.00am to 5.30pm or dusk, and in the summer until 6.00pm weekdays or 7.00pm weekends. Last admission half an hour before closing. Closed Christmas and New Year's Days, and Mondays during the winter

Prices: Adults £1.80 Monday to Saturday, £2.60 Sundays and Bank Holidays. Children half price, and under-5's free

Nappy Changing Facilities: Yes, in disabled toilets

Restaurant Facilities: Yes, open until half an hour before gardens closed, last orders half an hour before that

High Chairs: Yes

Nearby: Sandown Park Racecourse, and Esher town centre

The Whitbread Hop Farm

A S YOU APPROACH the Hop Farm you are rewarded with a spectacular and unmistakeable view of twenty huge oast houses silhouetted against the sky. In lovely countryside, and with several attractions for young children, the Farm is well worth a visit, especially in the summer, or when the weather is not too bad.

Once you have negotiated the reception area and shop (beware - the sweets are displayed in toddler-height pick and mix boxes, ideal for little fingers to explore whilst you are preoccupied paying the entrance fee!), you come out into a large grassy area, with gravelled paths leading between the oast houses, restaurant block and stable block. Start with the stable block, which is home to the enormous Shire horses, used in times past to deliver beer round London. Now these magnificent beasts are used for displays and processions, and you can see demonstrations of grooming, harnessing and driving. Watch them elegantly lifting their huge feathered feet and tossing their manes as they trot around the Farm. You can also go on short trailer rides, pulled by two horses, and look at the exhibits of old-fashioned drays. Unfortunately, children aren't allow to climb on these, which is a pity!

Across from the stables is an aviary, where you can get a good close-up look at several different kinds of birds of prey. Amazingly, owls and the like will sit quite motionless whilst children shriek and cavort a few feet away. The highlight of this part of the Farm is the flying displays, when owls are flown by a falconer. Much excitement can be had by even very young children, who can have a go wearing the falconer's glove and letting the owl fly onto their outstretched arm.

The Farm is host to an animal village, featuring a good range of small furry beasts - rabbits, guinea pigs, miniature ponies, goats and the like. These are nicely-kept in toddler-height pens, and provide the usual amusement for young children. Handling and touching opportunities are a bit limited though.

There is an adventure playground set a short walk away from the stables. This was quiet when we visited it, and our children had a great time. However, in more crowded periods it could be a bit boisterous, as there is no separate play area for the under-fives. The grounds are lovely, with plenty of picnic spots. If it rains, the hop museum inside some of the oast houses will amuse you for a little while, with its re-creation of the sights and sounds of the hop-picking heyday some fifty years ago.

The restaurant sells a good variety of hot meals, drinks, cakes, sandwiches and snacks. It is spacious, and has plenty of high chairs, although not all had straps.

FACT FILE

Address: The Whitbread Hop Farm, Beltring, Paddock Wood, Kent TN12 6PY

Telephone: 0622 872068

Directions: By car use the M20, and exit at junction 4 for Paddock Wood. Go on in towards Paddock Wood, following the signs to the Farm. By train to Paddock Wood from Charing Cross (trains on the hour and half hour, taking 50 minutes), and taxi from the station

Distance from SW London: 40 miles

Travel Time: 1 hour 30 minutes

Opening: Open all year, excluding Christmas, Boxing and New Years Days. Open 10.00am to 6.00pm in the summer and 10.00am to 4.00pm in the winter. Last admission one hour before closing

Prices: £4.95 adults, £3.00 children, under-5's free.

Nappy Changing Facilities: Yes

Restaurant Facilities: Yes

High Chairs: Yes

Nearby: Badsell Park Farm (see Animal Encounters section) is about five miles away

Wisley Royal Horticultural Society Gardens

*"With siver bells and cockle shells
and pretty maids all in a row"*

WISLEY GARDENS ARE a treat - a short drive down the A3, plenty of room for children to safely run about, and gorgeous gardens to admire at the same time. Although really an adult outing, children are very well accomodated for. However, be warned, if you are despairing over the state of your own tangled weed-bed, the displays of excellence will depress you even more!

The gardens are open all year, and offer something in all seasons. They are large enough to get away from everyone else if you want, and organised into over twenty different areas. There are heaps of wonderful lawns for running/crawling on, wide paths ideal for pushchairs (follow the wheelchair route to avoid any steps at all), and plenty of toddler-height walls for balancing practice. If you go there a lot (and it is quite possible to without getting bored), you will probably latch on to your own favourite places. Our favourites include the fruit fields and gardens, which display a huge variety of tree and soft fruits in all sorts of forms, from those suited to small gardens to awe-inspiring fan-trained trees. In case the fruit are proving too tempting to eager little fingers, it is worth remembering that all fruit in season is sold next to the car park from 1.00pm to 4.00pm every day. The Rock Garden, with its myriad of little paths and steps is also a favourite, along with the herbaceous borders and rose gardens (dazzling in summer) and the colourful trees and heather gardens in the Pinetum and Howard's Field.

Should your children tire of running in the gardens there is a pond and a lake across from the restaurant, which have ducks and huge goldfish lurking in the depths.

Although not really a wet-weather day out there is a large greenhouse, with hot, warm and cool plant displays, which is good to duck into if you find you need shelter!

Other facilities at Wisley are very good. There is a large cafe, with ample space, plenty of high chairs (though none with straps), and a terrace with tables overlooking a large lawned area - ideal in the summer. Hot and cold food, drinks, cakes and snacks are available in the cafe, and there is also a more formal restaurant next door. You are not permitted to picnic in the gardens, but there is a picnic area outside, near to the car park.

The shop next to the entrance is large and sells a good variety of National Trust-style gifts, books and stationery, though things aren't that cheap. There is also a very good plant shop for shrubs, trees, bedding plants, seeds etc. - take notes as you go round the gardens, and you can buy all the plants in the shop! (It might be better to leave your credit cards at home if you have a weakness for plant sales!)

FACT FILE

Address: Royal Horticultural Society Gardens, Wisley, Woking, Surrey GU23 6QB

Telephone: 0483 224234

Directions: By car, A3 from London, or M25 (exit 10), follow the signs just beyond the A3 and M25 intersection. By train from Waterloo or Clapham Junction to West Byfleet or Woking, and then a 2 or 3 mile taxi ride. Alternatively London Country Bus number 415 from Victoria

Distance from SW London: 20 miles

Travel Time: 30 minutes

Opening: 10.00am to 7.00pm in summer, 10.00am to sunset in winter. Monday to Saturday throughout the year (except Christmas Day). Open only to RHS members on Sundays

Prices: £4.50 adults, £1.75 children over 5 years old. Under-5's free. Free to RHS members

Nappy Changing Facilities: Yes, in the disabled toilet in the cafe

Restaurant Facilities: Yes

High Chairs: Yes

Nearby: The Angel Pub at Pyrford Lock on the River Wey offers pub food and welcomes families. See also Loseley Park Farm and Lockwood Donkey Sanctuary in the Animal Encounters section

LOOK! LOOK! LOOK ! - EXHIBITIONS AND THINGS TO SEE

Bekonscot Model Village

STEP BACK INTO the world of 1930's Agatha Christie England and visit this charming and intricate model village. The world in miniature on display is very tidy, and has efficient trains chugging about, cars with running boards, village corner shops and pubs, and wholesome, cheerful people. The detail is superb, with lots of humorous touches for adults (someone obviously had fun with the pub and shop names!), whilst there are a wealth of tiny features to amuse and fascinate children. Thoughtfully provided with picnic spots and an adventure playground too, Bekonscot makes an easy, fun day out. However, it is very popular in August, and can get crowded, whilst in the summer term there are often school visits in the morning, so it is probably best to time your arrival to coincide with lunch or just afterwards.

The village is set in one and a half acres of garden, with over one hundred and sixty buildings. A microcosm of idealised rural and village life is represented : shops, churches, schools, castles, a zoo, fishing harbour, fairground and racecourse, just to name a few of the features. A windy, narrow path snakes in and out and up and down through the village and surrounding 'countryside', providing good variety and the chance the see all the detail well, often at eye-level. It took us an hour to go all the way round once.

You have to follow the path and set route through, and with limited passing places, this means it may get frustrating at busy times. However, you can go round and round as many times as you like! The path was easily passable with our single buggy, but a double buggy would get stuck. You can use the (single) buggies provided at the entrance if your own pushchair is too wide.

A model railway with five trains busily runs around covering more or less the whole site. With several stations, lots of tunnels, viaducts and bridges, trains seem to pop up everywhere, and offer

great scope for distraction at any time. You can even see inside the life-sized signal box, where the signalman controls the points and signals with levers just like a real railway.

No village would be complete without its babbling brook and, true to life, you will find one at Bekonscot. The little stream merrily runs through part of the village, passing over a water wheel attached to a mill, and down over a waterfall into the 'sea', which, complete with pier, fishing harbour and lighthouse, is one of the most attractive features of the village. If you wonder what the wires running over the water are for, it is to discourage herons landing to make a meal of the huge carp lurking underwater!

The surrounding garden is wonderfully designed and maintained, with miniature trees and shrubs, and a profusion of rockery plants and flowers. Full-sized trees too, provide shade.

The village is provided with lots of picnic tables and benches. A refreshment kiosk is at the far end of the village, selling pizzas, burgers and hot dogs, as well as sandwiches, snacks, ices and teas. You can sit on tables and benches at the picnic area near the kiosk, but there is no inside seating there. However, there is a greenhouse near the main entrance with tables and seats, and you can sit there in wet or cold weather. As an alternative, Jung's cafe in Beaconsfield village (5 minutes walk from Bekonscot) serves hot meals and has high chairs and pleasant staff.

The adventure playground has good slides and climbing castles, with seating for parents and guardians. Its not huge, and may be hectic sometimes! A small gift shop at the entrance, located in an old railway carriage, has a reasonable range of small toys and gifts.

FACT FILE

Address: Bekonscot Model Village, Warwick Road, Beaconsfield, Bucks HP9 2PL

Telephone: 0494 672919

Directions: By car use the M40, leaving at junction 2, signposted for Beaconsfield and The Model Village. Either follow the Model Village signs around, or head straight into Beaconsfield Old and New villages. Bekonscot is in a side road behind Waitrose supermarket in Beaconsfield New village. By train from Marylebone to Beaconsfield (8-10 minutes walk)

Distance from SW London: 30 miles

Travel Time: 50 minutes to 1 hour

Opening: Every day from 10.00am to 5.00pm. From mid-February until the end of October

Prices: £3.00 adults, £1.50 children. Under-3's free. Group discounts are available

Nappy Changing Facilities: Yes

Restaurant Facilities: Limited

High Chairs: No

Nearby: Hell Fire Caverns, West Wycombe Caves, near High Wycombe would make a spooky place to visit (0494 33739), or try Burnham Beeches, a lovely picnic spot nearby (follow signs to Wooburn Green)

Brighton Sea Life Centre

B RIGHTON IS ALWAYS a fun place to visit with young children - not only is there the sea (albeit with a pebbly beach), and grand pier to stroll along, but also you can wander through the maze of little shops in the Lanes area (behind the sea front), or have a picnic and cup of tea in the delightful park next to the Pavilion buildings. The Sea Life Centre, next to the pier, is completely indoors and means that Brighton is still worth a day trip even in wet or cold weather.

If you and your children are not completely fazed by practically rubbing noses with a shark or tickling a sting ray, then you will have a wonderful time at the Centre. You start by walking through a series of aquariums in the elegantly-restored Victorian display area. Huge fish glide literally inches away in floor to ceiling tanks, which are subtly-lit and ingeniously modelled to re-create the sea-bottom. Wrecks, sunken treasure and ominous caverns abound. The size of the tanks and the well-provided viewing platforms mean that children (even those in pushchairs) can get a really good view.

These displays open out into a wider area, where a sandy sea-bed has been re-created on one side, and an old harbour the other. The sandy sea-bed is teeming with graceful sting rays, which rear up out of the water almost as if they are saying hello. For the brave (or foolhardy) there are instructions given on how to stroke the rays. Apparently these two to three foot long creatures are very gentle and do not sting unless you tread on them. Note that over-enthusiastic little hands would not be able to reach the rays on their own - if you wanted your children to touch the rays you would have to lift them over the guard rail. The old harbour is full of creaking boards and sounds of seagulls, with plenty of huge crabs dancing over the sea-bed. Again, the floor level displays mean that everyone gets a good view.

Walk on through more tanks displaying deeper-water creatures, such as octopus and lobsters. Some of these tanks have special viewing 'bubbles', which enable you to feel that you are in the water with the beastees! The *piece de resistance*, though, is the underwater tunnel, which offers superb close-up views of British sharks, more sting rays, and conger eels. We were there at feeding time, which was fascinating, but not for the squeamish! Suffice to say, much enjoyment was had by all as these mysterious creatures glided and cavorted above and around our heads.

The Centre is well-set up with other facilities for young children. There is a small soft play area, next to the sandy sea-shore display, a video unit, and plenty of excellent audio-visual displays. Sammy's cafe sells a variety of hot meals and snacks, and has a limited number of high chairs. It caters for birthday parties if you book in advance. There is also a shop which sells a good variety of fishy-style gifts, toys and sweets. Feeding of the denizens of the deep takes place twice a day, although it is not always the creatures in the tunnel.

The whole Centre is easily accessible with a pushchair. Don't be deterred at the entrance by the long flight of steps down, there is a small entrance for disabled leading directly off the seafront at the side, with no steps to negotiate at all!

FACT FILE

Address: Brighton Sea Life Centre, Marine Parade, Brighton

Telephone: 0273 604233 (24 hour information line),

Directions: Brighton is only just over an hour on the train, with frequent services from Victoria or Clapham Junction. Brighton station is about a 15 minute walk from the Sea Life Centre. Alternatively, by car, take the M23, and A23 straight to Brighton and head for the sea front

Distance from SW London: 50 miles

Travel Time: 1 hour to 1 hour 30 minutes

Opening: 10.00am to 5.00pm every day, except Christmas Day. Later in the summer

Prices: Adults £4.50, children £3.25 Under-4's free

Nappy Changing Facilities: Yes

Restaurant Facilities: Yes

High Chairs: Yes

Nearby: Brighton Toy and Model Museum, next to the train station, is open daily from 10.00am to 5.00pm Mondays to Saturday, and 11.00am to 5.00pm on Sundays. During the summer the Volks electric railway on the sea front offers short rides along the coast. There are plenty of shops, parks and restaurants in the town, including lots of fish and chip shops!

Gatwick Airport and Zoo

IF YOU'VE EVER been frustrated waiting around for planes, a day out to Gatwick airport must seem the most unlikely way to have a good time. However, read on, because, for children, there is a reasonable amount to see and do at Gatwick, and it has the added benefit for brain-dead parents or carers of being self-contained and *completely indoors*. Plus, you may not be aware that there is a small zoo nearby, so if it does stop raining you can always go there too.

The most hassle-free thing to do is to drive to the short-term car park at the new North terminal. You can park there for about £1.00 an hour. (Of course you can always get the train from Clapham Junction or Victoria for a real action-packed planes and trains day out!). Take the lifts into the departure hall. There you can mingle with smartly-dressed business people (remember that?), exotic travellers from far-flung (warm, no doubt) places, and other people like yourself with nothing better to do. Inside the departure hall there are plenty of shops, notably Boots, the Body Shop, and WH Smiths, and a wealth of restaurants and snack bars. For older children there is even a flight simulator.

Once you get bored, take the transit train to the South terminal. This short aerial train ride offers views of the airport from large picture windows. In the South terminal there is one of those moving 'traveolator' things, which provides a fair degree of amusement for toddlers (keep hold of children, though, as it could be dangerous). More shops, business people, and travellers can be found inside the South terminal. However, at one end of the terminal you can take the lifts to the top floor, and the spectator viewing gallery. This is on the roof, and offers a wonderful view of the main runway, as well as one of the main loading and parking bays. You can watch, hear and smell the huge jets manoeuvre out and onto the runway, before launching themselves skywards, and disappearing. The spectator shop, recently re-furbished, sells cards, model planes, and information for plane freaks.

If you have time, and energy, you could visit the Charlwood Zoo, which is about 3 miles from the airport. Although, not really a major excursion in its own right, it makes a valuable extra diversion if you are in the vicinity. To get there drive past the North terminal, and follow signs to Crawley and Redhill. The zoo is signposted with brown cockatoo signs from just beyond the airport. It is a small zoo and aviary, manageable in about an hour to an hour and a half. You can buy food for the animals at the entrance (35p a cup), and watch the monkeys playing on a moated island with tree ropes, swings and a house. There is a small adventure playground (which can be a bit muddy), and a picnic area, as well as a little cafe selling sandwiches and other light refreshments.

FACT FILE

Address: Gatwick Airport, Crawley, Surrey and Gatwick Zoo, Russ Hill, Charlwood, Surrey RH6 0EG

Telephone: Airport 0293 535353, Zoo 0293 862312

Directions: Gatwick airport exit off the M23 and follow signs. Train to Gatwick airport from Victoria or Clapham Junction (comes into the South terminal). Use the Network South Central service, rather than the Gatwick Express - its cheaper, and only a few minutes slower. Open top buses numbers 88 and 439 go to Gatwick Zoo from the airport onSaturdays, Sundays and Bank Holidays. Ring the Zoo or telephone 0293 617111 for information

Distance from SW London: 30 miles

Travel Time: 1 hour

Opening: Airport, all times. Spectator viewing from 8.00am to 7.00pm in the summer, and 9.00am to 4.00pm in the winter. The Zoo opens every day from March to October inclusive, 10.30am to 6.00pm, and weekends and school holidays from November to February, 10.30am to dusk. Last admission an hour before closing

Prices: Airport spectator area 60p adults, 30p children, free for under-5's. Zoo £3.50 adults, £2.50 children 3 to 14 years

Nappy Changing Facilities: Plenty in the airport, none in the Zoo

Restaurant Facilities: Yes

High Chairs: Plenty in airport, not in the Zoo

Nearby: The North Downs, around Leith Hill has some lovely walks and picnic spots

Kempton Park Races

"I bet my money on a bobtailed nag, doo-da, doo-da"

AND THEY'RE OFF! and so were we for a day at the races. Horse racing is probably one of the few major spectator sports that are compatible with young children. For all the hustle and bustle, there is a friendly atmosphere and you will find that many people bring children. At Kempton Park they have recognised this and invested in a creche, so that little ones can take a break from the afternoon's entertainment if they want.

Access could not be much easier - one popular way is to come by car with a jolly good picnic, and park in the middle of the course - wandering to the rails for each race as it comes along. There is also a dedicated railway station right by the course, with frequent services from Waterloo on race days.

Once on the course, mingle with the crowds in the Silver Ring Enclosure. Between races there is an ever-changing kaleidoscope of people from all walks of life, bookies shaving their odds (get your children to research the best odds amongst the bookies), 'tic-tac men' signalling the odds to unseen watchers, and horses warming up on the course. Or go round the back of the stands to the paddock, where the horses begin their pre-race preparation. Usually you can get close enough for a really good look at these magnificent beasts, all gleaming coats and slender, muscled legs.

Try to place a bet on each race - it makes it much more fun. You will find that bookies in the Silver Ring Enclosure expect a minimum bet of £2.00. No need to spend the morning in the Public Library comparing the odds and boning up on the colours of the jockeys' silks, however. Our experience is that any daily newspaper carries extensive discussion of the relative merits of the main contenders, enabling you to carry on a seemingly knowledgeable conversation before making your choice. You can also buy programmes on course which carry quite a lot of information, if you want to really get into it. Children love to get involved, they can see the horses in the paddock and choose the one they like best, or choose a favourite number or colour.

When you have exhausted the fun to be had in the Silver Ring, there is often further entertainment to be had on the racecourse. Sponsors often arrange exhibitions and demonstrations.

If your children are very young or simply get tired and want a break there is a free creche. It is located in the Silver Ring Enclosure, behind the main stand. It is quite simple, but adequately equipped, and there are plenty of enthusiastic and willing helpers. It is rather small though, with a capacity of about 20 children. You can leave children from 0 to eight years old, and for up to an hour on busy days, longer when it is quiet. It is probably a good idea to ensure you get there early if you definitely want to leave your children there for a period.

Other facilities for children are fairly limited. Toilets are basic, and do not boast nappy changing facilities, though you can change a nappy in the creche, even if there is not room to leave your child. The eating and drinking places are take-away bars and caravans. Great for slumming it with chips and tomato ketchup, but be warned that there are no high chairs or sit-down cafes in the Silver Ring Enclosure.

Excitement always runs high for the King George VI Stake on Boxing Day (you know, the one that Desert Orchid always used to win) and joining the big crowd there to eat your turkey sandwiches makes a great change. There are meetings throughout the year of course; a warm sunny day can be wonderful for a relaxed picnic. At the height of summer, there are evening meetings (some with fireworks), with the last race at about 9.00pm. The creche is available for these evening meetings too.

One final tip - leave before the last race if you have travelled by car. The car parks exit onto the narrow roads around Sunbury which soon jam with the sudden heavy traffic flow at the end of the day's racing. It can take over an hour to get out of the car park if you do try to leave when everyone else does.

FACT FILE

Address: Kempton Park Racecourse, Sunbury on Thames, Middlesex TW16 5AQ

Telephone: 0932 782292

Directions: A316 from west London to Sunbury, then follow the signs for the racecourse. Kempton Park is just off the A308. By train from Waterloo on race days

Distance from SW London: 20 miles

Travel Time: 45 minutes

Opening: 1 or 2 meetings most months, more in the summer when there are evening meetings too. Telephone in advance to see which days. Most afternoon meetings start at 2.00pm, and evening ones at 6.00pm. You can usually go in about an hour before the first race

Prices: Silver Ring £6.00 on feature days, £4.00 otherwise. Grandstand £13.00 on feature days, £10.00 otherwise. Children under 16 years old free

Nappy Changing Facilities: None, except in creche

Restaurant Facilities: Takeaway only

High Chairs: None

Syon Butterfly House and Park

ON A COLD or dull day, a visit to the Butterfly House, with its warm, humid atmosphere and brightly-coloured tropical flowers, takes some beating. When you first walk in, it takes a few minutes before your eyes adjust to the fact that there are butterflies everywhere. Fluttering through the air, sitting lazily stretching their wings on paths and foliage, hidden in leaves, big ones, small ones, if you start trying to point out every single one you see you will rapidly go into manic overdrive! Although on bright and sunny days you will see more butterflies, even on a dull day the sheer number there is quite amazing - a minimum of 500 on display at any one time, with up to sixty different species. Of course the colours are fantastic: vivid oranges, yellows, viridians, in a huge variety of stripes, spots and leopard skins. And as for size, ranging from about an inch across, to the huge Owl butterflies (about five inches) and Giant Atlas Moths (a stupendous seven inches).

The butterflies are all housed in a large greenhouse, which is subdivided into several sections. There is a small stream running through, with little bridges and pools with terrapins and fish. All captivate small children. The wishing well, which encouraged them to roll coins down to land into the water with a satisfying 'plop', was found to be highly diverting! There are archways laden with tropical blossom, pergolas, and benches where you can sit and watch, and try to match the butterflies you can see with those on the identification charts. Identification leaflets are on sale in the shop for 60p each, or you can use the boards inside the butterfly house. Exotic fragrances meander in the heavy air. The emerging cages near the entrance give the chance to watch butterflies coming out from the pupal stages, and if you may also see caterpillars on the underside of some leaves (staff are happy to help out with finding caterpillars, and with identification problems!).

Most of the butterflies are in the tropical sections. However, from May to September, British butterflies are displayed in an adjoining area. At the exit is a small insect gallery - giant millipedes, lizards,

tarantulas and the like. Toddlers really needed to be lifted up for a good view here. There is also a very good shop, with small toys, wall charts and books, on a general 'nature' theme.

A visit to the Butterfly House may take from one to two hours. However, there is quite a lot more to do in the vicinity so a day passes easily. Syon Park is worth visiting at the same time as the butterflies - fifty five acres of Capability Brown landscaped parkland, which make a very pleasant walk at any time of year. There is a large lake running through the middle (beware - it is unfenced), with a few ducks, many fine and interesting trees, and paths suitable for pushchairs. A short miniature railway runs at weekends and bank holidays during the summer, and there is plenty of room for a picnic. Should it rain, you could always retreat to the Conservatory! Although probably not suitable for children, Syon House itself is open from Easter to September, and there is also a large garden centre, National Trust shop, art shop and wholefood shop, as well as restaurant facilities. In the summer the Koi shop often has exhibits of huge fish in large pools outside.

FACT FILE

Address: London Butterfly House, Syon Park, Brentford, Middlesex

Telephone: 081 560 7272

Directions: By car, take the South Circular to Kew Bridge, then turn left down the A315 towards Twickenham. Signposted 'Syon House'. By rail from Waterloo or Clapham Junction, to Kew Bridge station, then 237 or 267 bus to Brentlea Gate (50 yards to pedestrian entrance)

Distance from SW London: 12 miles

Travel Time: 30 to 45 minutes

Opening: Summer 10.00am to 5.00pm, winter 10.00am to 3.30pm. Every day except Christmas and Boxing Days. Syon Park Gardens open 10.00am to 6.00pm or dusk, seven days a week

Prices: Butterfly House £2.60 adults, £1.60 children. Under-3's free. Family ticket (2 adults, up to 4 children) £6.90

Nappy Changing Facilities: Table in ladies toilets in Patio Cafe, adjacent to park entrance

Restaurant Facilities: Yes, in the Patio cafe

High Chairs: Two - one with straps

Nearby: Kew Gardens (see The Sun Has Got His Hat On section), Kew Bridge Steam museum (weekends only)

SOMEWHAT HISTORICAL - CASTLES AND COTTAGES

Fort Luton and Kent Life Museum

"Slugs and snails and puppy dogs' tails. . ."

FORT LUTON IS an 'experience' - great if you like dark, dank tunnels replete with ghastlies and ghouls. Unfortunately many children do! Built in the 19th century the Fort's remaining buildings are tunnels and underground arches in what I can only describe as 'pill-box' military architecture style i.e. not particularly gracious. However, it has now been restored and re-opened, and filled with a real 'dogs dinner' of models and relics. The sort that many young children find absolutely fascinating (although adults will probably find quite repellent!). Home-made models, models rescued from TV and film sets, models discovered lurking in garages and attics, model railways, model villages, robots, monsters, space invaders - you name it, they are all scattered around the Fort somewhere! There are some serious museums too, notably a doll and toy museum, and a penny arcade (come with old 10p pieces if you want to see some of the displays in action). This extraordinary melange seems to keep children whooping with delight for hours.

Apart from the indoor 'attractions' there are several things to do out in the four-and-a-half-acre grounds - an adventure playground, pets corner (with the ugliest turkey I've ever seen), duck pond, moat walk and picnic areas.

The facilities are adequate, but a bit basic. There is a nappy changing mat in the Ladies loo, a cafe serving hot food and cakes and with one high chair, and a gift shop.

The Fort makes a weird day out, but to make it worth the trip from London you should combine it with a visit to the nearby Kent Life Museum near Maidstone, which with its fresh air and open spaces will be a good antidote to Fort Luton's subterranean tunnels. The Museum is set in 26 acres of rural land overlooking

the River Medway, and consists of restored buildings, exhibitions and displays which recreate and glorify rural life in times past in this county, the 'Garden of England'. It runs alongside Allington Lock where boats are moored and ducks paddle leisurely. It has a quiet rural feel and tranquil atmosphere, especially mid-week.

Our children's favourites are the re-constructed hop-pickers huts where adults can wonder at the primitive conditions endured by the annual influx of hop-pickers from London whilst children play house in their shacks. Then there is the 18th century Vale Farm barn which is crammed with displays to keep young children enthralled - farm implements, machinery, and tractors. Traditional crafts such as carpentry, weaving, blacksmithing, and potting are regularly demonstrated, whilst seasonal farming activities are always on show - the grand finale being the hop-picking which takes place over the Harvest Weekend, and which visitors can arrange to participate in, if the fancy really takes them!

Being a farm there are animals to admire too, notably Rosie the Shire Horse, lambs, goats, rabbits and guinea pigs. These are all in a farmyard, with plenty of stroking and holding opportunities. There is also a wooden pig - a popular scrambling post.

The 'Darling Buds of May' exhibition has lorries and a tractor, as well as re-creations of the Larkin family rooms - probably a bit over the heads of most young children, but ours enjoyed clambering over the truck!

The tea-rooms are very pleasant, licensed, and offer hot meals, snacks, ice-creams and drinks, which you can eat inside or take out into the gardens. There is a designated picnic area next to the tea-rooms, but there is lots of space to have a picnic anywhere in the fields.

FACT FILE

Address: Fort Luton, Magpie Hall Road, Chatham, Kent
and Kent Life Museum, Lock Lane, Sandling,
Maidstone, Kent ME14 3AU

Telephone: Fort Luton 0634 813969, Museum 0622 763936

Directions: For the Fort the M2 motorway, junction 3, the
Chatham exit. Fork right after Toys R Us, and follow signs to
the Fort. The Museum is off the M20 motorway (use junction 6
and head for Maidstone on the A229). Signposted from the
motorway. Train to Chatham from Victoria, and bus numbers
164 and 64 from Chatham's Pentagon bus station to Magpie
Hall Road and Fort Luton. Train to Maidstone from Victoria,
regular buses from Maidstone East to the Museum, or taxi from
the station (about 2 or 3 miles)

Distance from SW London: 40 miles

Travel Time: 1 hour 30 minutes

Opening: Fort Luton, every day except Christmas and
Boxing Day, 10.00am to 4.00pm or dusk weekdays, 10.00am
to 6.00pm weekends. Museum, from Easter to the end of
October, every day from 10.30am to 5.30pm

Prices: Fort Luton £2.50 adults, £1.75 children aged 4 and
over. The Museum £3.00 adults, £1.50 children. Free for
under 5's

Nappy Changing Facilities: Yes

Restaurant Facilities: Yes

High Chairs: Yes

Nearby: Chatham's Historic Dockyards have recently been
restored and re-opened, and offer an insight into naval,
military and industrial history. They are open every day from end
of March to end of October 10.00am to 5.00pm, and during
the winter open Wednesday, Saturday and Sunday 10.00am to
4.30pm. There is a Mad Hatters Tea Party at Easter, and
heavy horse waggon ride tours during the summer (0634 812551)

Greenwich - Cutty Sark and Maritime Museum

"All hands on deck!"

S HIVER ME TIMBERS, landlubbers!! Standing on the wooden decks of the Cutty Sark at Greenwich, and imagining the freezing waves crashing over them at 45 degrees is enough to make you feel sea-sick, let alone think about climbing aloft to wrestle with salt-encrusted ropes and sails! But that was life aboard this famous sailing ship, now dry-docked in Greenwich Harbour, and, together with the many other local attractions, it makes for a splendid day out.

Greenwich is easy and quick to get to, both in the car and by public transport. If you do come by car, be warned that parking can be difficult - try around Maritime Museum or Cutty Sark jetty. Also Greenwich is popular with tourists, and often busy. It is best to get there in the morning, see the Cutty Sark and wander round the streets first, before escaping to the quieter Maritime Museum and Greenwich Park for lunch and the afternoon.

The Cutty Sark is the only surviving tea clipper (i.e. a sailing boat to you and me), launched in 1869 for the tea trade, and later used on the wool route to Australia. When was built she was faster than steam ships, and you'll find lots of friendly guides on board who will willingly tell you (as well as many other things) that this was due to her sails, which were equal in area to 11 tennis courts (a rather bizzare unit of measurement!). Now, with her towering main mast and complex rigging, she is a majestic sight, with wide decks which our children found to be great for tearing about on. They were also thrilled by all the steep ladder stairs, and awkward little doorways. The ship's Golden Rule of 'one hand for the ship and one hand for yourself' is worth remembering! However, the ship is absolutely no good for pushchairs, so take backpacks for non-walkers.

The ship is filled 'plumb to the gun'ls' with exciting things for young children - highlights being the lurid figurehead collection in the lower hold, the Captain's cabin, the rope-handled buckets on deck, the massive wheel (actually used to steer round Cape Horn), and the crew quarters and bunks (trying them for size was very popular). On some Sundays you may be lucky enough to catch a troupe of shanty singers whose lively songs make a great atmosphere. (The words have obviously been cleaned up from the original bawdy sailors' ditty!) There is also a ship shop, selling charts, posters, models and guides.

The nearby Maritime Museum has lovely grounds you can walk round for free, with massive 32 pounder guns (great to climb on) and a playground with a very popular wooden 'barge'. Inside the museum are exhibitions of Britain's maritime history - model ships, barges, Nelson's uniform and so on. The pirates' exhibition is tremendous for children: it has been re-opened by popular demand, but is only temporary unfortunately. On Saturday and Sunday afternoons Captain Tugboat does storytelling sessions on the 1905 steam paddle tugboat.

Greenwich has lots of other things to do. The craft market on Saturdays and Sundays has a myriad of brightly coloured stalls selling clothes, wooden toys, and all sort of other, good-quality craftware. It can be crowded. Greenwich Park is extensive, has good views, and is very hilly and great for running up and down. Donkey rides are available at the top of park (Shooters Hill) on some days, and you can also visit the Old Royal Observatory which has a huge digital clock, and a hands-on science station for children. There is a cafe in the park. Guided walks around Greenwich, lasting about an hour to an hour and a half, are run by the Tourist Office in Greenwich Church Street (081 858 6169, prices from £2.50, under-14's free).

There are plenty of choices for eating in Greenwich. We recommend the Bosun's Whistle Restaurant in the Maritime Museum which is not too busy, and has some high chairs with straps. It offers hot snacks, cakes, drinks, ices and sandwiches. The Pier cafe on the harbour is cheap for drinks and snacks, and you can watch the boats going up and down the Thames.

FACT FILE

Address: Cutty Sark, King William Walk, Greenwich, London SE10 9HT

Telephone: 081 858 3445 (Cutty Sark)
081 858 4422, and 081 312 6602 (Maritime Museum)

Directions: By car use the South Circular, A202, following signs to Greenwich on the A206. By rail, frequent trains from Charing Cross, Waterloo East, Cannon Street and London Bridge (about a 20 minute ride). Boats from Westminster, Charing Cross or Tower piers, 20 minutes ride, about every 30 minutes (telephone 071 930 4097)

Distance from SW London: 15 miles

Travel Time: 45 minutes

Opening: Cutty Sark, every day except 24th, 25th and 26th December. Weekdays 10.00am to 6.00pm summer (April to September), and 10.00am to 5.00pm winter. Sundays and Bank Holidays 12noon to 5.00pm (to 6.00pm in summer). Maritime Museum 10.00am to 6.00pm Monday to Saturday (until 5.00pm in winter), and 12noon to 6.00pm Sundays (2.00pm to 5.00pm in the winter)

Prices: Cutty Sark, Adults £3.25, children £2.75, under-7's free. Museum, adults £3.75, children £2.75, under-7's free. Family passport tickets, allowing admission to all Greenwich's main attractions for 2 adults and up to 5 children cost £14.50

Nappy Changing Facilities: Yes (Maritime Museum)

Restaurant Facilities: Yes

High Chairs: Yes

Leeds Castle

WHO HASN'T HEARD of Leeds castle, or the 'the loveliest castle in the world' as it is often referred to? Although young children may be oblivious to the undoubted beauty of the castle and its setting, there is plenty for them to see in the grounds whilst you muse romantically, and lots of space for them to run about. A word of caution though, there are several unfenced streams and lakes in the grounds, which, albeit extremely scenic, do mean that you have to keep your eye on toddlers. However, on a sunny day, it would take a lot to beat a visit here.

From the entrance and car park follow the path through the woodland garden to the castle itself - about a twenty minute walk. The path is well-maintained, with several little wooden bridges, and easily negotiable with a pushchair. Carpeted with daffodils and narcissi in the spring; the gardens are very attractive at any time of the year. Our children were thrilled by the Duckery -an area of small ponds and streams created out of the River Len, and full of all sorts of wildfowl roaming freely on the banks and in the water. Try telling your children to not chase the ducks! (we weren't very successful!). A certain amount of agility and nimble footedness on your part may be required here if you don't want an extremely wet and muddy child.

When you are about three quarters of the way through the gardens you get your first view of the castle rising mysteriously and majestically from the waters of the lake. It is a wonderful sight. As you walk up to the castle entrance you can decide whether you want to go in or not. A tour of the various rooms and galleries (including state rooms, bedrooms, a wine cellar, and chapel) with the associated halls, staircases, corridors and courtyards would probably take about an hour, and is unlikely to appeal to young children. You are not permitted to take pushchairs inside - you must leave them at the castle entrance, where someone will keep an eye on them.

We stayed outside in the sun and fresh air. Carry on walking beyond the castle and along the side of the lakes to a visitor area which has special attractions for children: the most interesting being the aviary and maze. The aviary has a host of merrily squawking parakeets, cockatoos and parrots (or are they all the same thing?!). On the whole children can easily see into the cages and get a good look at the birds. There are also huge carp and terrapins in pools - much admired by our children.

No pushchairs are allowed into the maze, so be prepared to carry your children or persuade them to walk. It is definitely worth going in, if you can manage it. The maze is a mass of hedged paths, leading, if you are successful at finding your way, to a mound in the middle. This is a great vantage point to jeer at members of your party who haven't got there yet. The mound is, in fact, a hollow dome containing a grotto, which provides an exciting alternative way out of the maze. Although the steps and corridors are very uneven, we had great fun descending into its gloomy depths, and the imaginative and surprising decor (serpents, underworld beasts, skeletons and the like) provoked shrills of glee.

The Culpepper garden is also worth a stroll. It is a small walled garden next to the aviary with a profusion of old English cottage garden flowers and herbs. The brick paths and low box-hedged flower beds are a delight to walk in, or run around playing hide and seek in, depending on your preference (and age!). Finally, there is a greenhouse, which is warm and full of exotic blooms, and a vineyard, home to the vines which produce the Leeds Castle wine.

Refreshments are provided in Fairfax Hall, which is a spacious and magnificently-timbered 17th century barn located half way between the castle and aviary. Hot and cold food, and teas are served, at reasonable prices. The courtyard outside is very pleasant, with benches and tables should you wish to sit and enjoy the sunshine. You can picnic in a designated picnic spot near the main entrance to the garden.

A gift shop, bookshop, and nappy changing facilities are set around the sides of the Fairfax Hall courtyard.

The castle puts on special events throughout the year. The Easter Egg hunt through the grounds sounds like great fun for children, and they would probably also enjoy the Hot Air Balloon festival in June (check precise dates).

FACT FILE

Address: Leeds Castle, Maidstone, Kent ME17 IPL

Telephone: 0891 800680

Directions: By car, 4 miles east of Maidstone, just off junction 8 of the M20. Signposted from the motorway. By train from Victoria to Bearsted station, with a ten minute coach transfer from Bearsted station on castle open days. All-inclusive tickets (train, coach and admission) available from rail operator (071 620 1032 for information). You can also get a National Express coach from Victoria Station, (071 730 0202)

Distance from SW London: 40 miles

Travel Time: 1 hour 30 minutes

Opening: All year. From 10.00am to 5.00pm from March onwards, and from 10.00am to 3.00pm in winter. Closed the day before special events

Prices: Park only £5.50 adults, £3.30 children 5 years and above. Free for under-5's. Castle and park £7.00 adults, £4.80 children 5 and over. Family tickets available

Nappy Changing Facilities: Yes

Restaurant Facilities: Yes

High Chairs: Yes

Nearby: The Kent Life Museum (see previous entry in this section). Maidstone's Mote Park Leisure Centre with Jungle Gym and Ice-Hills (a toboggan run for 3 to 5 year-olds). Creche on weekdays (0622 759615)

Weald and Downland Open Air Museum

ALTHOUGH 'RURAL ARCHITECTURE' may not sound like the most thrilling way to amuse young children, this award-winning museum falls into the category of 'fascinating for adults plus safe letting-off steam potential for children' and makes a great day out.

This 'museum' is unlike any other museum you may have visited. For a start it is in the open air - 55 acres of gorgeous countryside to be precise, and you (and, in particular, your children) are free to wander, explore and play hide and seek without fear of breaking anything. The museum consists of over 30 rescued historical buildings from the South of England, which have been faithfully and meticulously re-erected. The result is a delightful and informative taste of what the environment of rural and small town England used to be like to live and work in.

There are two suggested routes to follow through the museum, and you can comfortably fit in both in a day, or just about in one afternoon. The shorter, red, route takes about half an hour to one hour, and takes in the museum shop (selling gifts, children's colouring books, posters and booklets), several re-created artisan workshops, a working water mill, and mill pond, as well as other shops, houses and other buildings from the 15th to 19th century. Highlights of this route include the brick house, where you can play making patterns with traditional bricks, and the water mill, where you can watch the wheat being ground between huge grit millstones into creamy coloured stoneground flour. Both the end product, the flour, and the ingoing wheat are on sale at the mill. The latter is sold as duck food (25p a bag), for the many varieties of ducks and geese who live noisily on the adjacent mill pond.

The longer, green, route takes anything upwards of an hour and a half, and is a lovely walk through the valley bottom and surrounding woodland. Like the red route you can do it with a pushchair. It takes in traditional cottages and barns, a village school, and shepherds' huts, as well as a re-created charcoal burners camp,

and the impressive medieval Bayleaf farm. The farm in particular is well worth a visit, with its authentic wood fire in the centre of the hall, where candle-making was in progress when we visited. It also has traditional farm gardens and animals, including huge wallowing pigs, and William, the Shire horse.

There is a refreshment area near the mill pond, selling soup, light lunches, bread rolls (home made with the flour from the mill), tea and cakes. It is closed November to March. You can eat inside a nearby cottage, with open window slats letting in sparrows, which our daughter had great fun chasing! There are also plenty of picnic tables and benches around, or you may eat your own food anywhere in the grounds, except inside the houses (it attracts mice).

Because you can always duck into a nearby building this is a day out with wet weather potential, although if it is really pouring continuously children's opportunities to run about outside may be a bit curtailed! When we went in October there was a lovely smell of wood smoke drifting through the air, and lots of autumn leaves to kick through. It can get busy in the summer, as it is popular with school parties, but there is a lot of space to escape into, and after about 3.00pm they all go home, apparently!

FACT FILE

Address: Weald & Downland Open Air Museum, Singleton, Chichester, West Sussex PO18 0EU

Telephone: 0243 811348

Directions: A3, then A286 to Midhurst and Chichester. Signposted from Singleton village (midway between Midhurst and Chichester). By train to Chichester from Waterloo, then number 260 bus to Singleton, which runs about every 40 minutes

Distance from SW London: 50 miles

Travel Time: 1 hour 30 minutes

Opening: Every day in the summer, from 11.00am to 6.00pm. Check in advance for winter opening, as times are changing

Prices: £4.20 adults, £2.70 children 5 years and older. Under-5's free. Family tickets £11.00 (2 adults, 2 children)

Nappy Changing Facilities: Yes, in toilets by car park at entrance

Restaurant Facilities: Yes

High Chairs: No

Nearby: In Singleton village the Horse and Groom pub has a family room and play area. Midhurst is a pretty, small town with plenty of tea shops. Goodwood Racecourse is within a few miles of the museum (telephone 0243 774107 for racedays)

THE SUN HAS GOT HIS HAT ON - WALKS AND PICNICS

Clifton Hampden

"All was a-shake and a-shiver, glints and gleams and sparkles,
Rustle and swirl, chatter and bubble"

REMEMBER THOSE LAZY summer days, dangling your feet in a cool river as the sun baked down? Clifton Hampden will bring all those memories flooding back - playing ball in a river meadow, eating sandwiches and drinking fizzy drinks. The Thames curves lazily through the bridge, the meadow spreads out on one side while the village gardens and small coppices cover the slight scarp on the other side. To the south lie the rolling Sinodun Hills, outriders for the Chilterns, dominated by the ancient site of Wittenham Clumps.

Clifton Hampden is a few miles south of Oxford, four miles east of Abingdon along the A415. There is a small village with 2 pubs (The Plough beside the A415 and the Barley Mow) and a village shop of the type which is rapidly becoming extinct (BEWARE! ice-cream may be available. . .). Turning south off the A415 (signposted Long Wittenham), you rapidly cross the old bridge, with its many arches. The road swings to the right, round a picturesque thatched pub, the Barley Mow, on your right and a car park appears on your left. Leave the car here and walk back along the road to the bridge. It is a popular spot with local people and you should have no trouble finding the stile through to the meadow on your right (just a couple of hundred yards from the car park). Immediately you are in a broad grassy area - pitch up here if you wish, or walk on along the riverside towpath (public right of way) and stop further down. Some fields will have cows grazing, but they generally seem incurious of their visitors. The river bank here has been eroded to form a series of miniscule 'coves', many of which

boast sand or fine gravel bottoms. Ideal for a little paddling - but do be careful. The river generally runs slower and calmer on this side but the Thames is a powerful river and children could easily be swept away.

There are few specific facilities for families - but what do you need in a rural picnic spot? There are toilets in the car park, but they are basic and we have found them vandalised on occasion. Both pubs welcome families and have outside areas. The village shop stocks basic necessities, soft drinks etc. .

For a wider selection of goodies Abingdon is probably your best bet. Indeed, you could do worse than plan to spend part of your day there. It has many attractive buildings in the town centre (pedestrianised) and a wide choice of pubs and restaurants. Other local places to visit include the medieval Abbey in nearby Dorchester and the museum in Long Wittenham. However I suspect that you will just want to spread out your blanket, get out the bat and ball and open up the hamper for a day of bliss on the river bank.

FACT FILE

Address: Clifton Hampden, Long Wittenham, Oxon

Directions: The easiest way to get there is probably up the M40 as far as junction 7 (Milton Common) taking the A329 to Stadhampton and thence to Clifton Hampden either via Drayton St. Leonards or via Chiselhampton and Golden Balls

Distance from SW London: 60 miles

Travel Time: 1 hour 30 minutes

Nappy Changing Facilities: No

Restaurant Facilities: The Barley Mow and Plough pubs

High Chairs: No

Nearby: Oxford, Medieval abbey at Dorchester

Kew Gardens

IF YOU THINK that the Royal Botanic Gardens at Kew are just for ardent plant spotters discussing the merits of different chrysanthemum species, think again, because they are ideal for a day's picnic, and very easy to get to, both by car and by public transport. One of Kew's strongest points is that it is dog free, which must make it one of the largest pooh-free areas that you can find. Despite being very popular at weekends, you can still find far-flung corners that are practically deserted, and in the week - well, you will almost find the whole gardens at your disposal.

A mixture of wide grassed areas and woodland, the gardens are very extensive - you'd be hard pushed to cover everywhere in a day. Although there are some formal flower displays most of the gardens are wild in character, but do have lovely wide pushchair-friendly footpaths. There are no nasty 'Keep off the grass' notices, and you can romp at will through shady dells and woody glens. Dotted around are information boards to help you gen up on your general knowledge skills (do you know how many oak trees it took to build a sailing galleon, for example?). Older children get a lot out of these boards. At the quieter, far side of the gardens the paths border onto the banks of the Thames, with the requisite fisherman and the occasional rowing eight.

The leaflet you are given at the entrance marks three suggested walks - try the West walk, the quietest, with several little shelters and alcoves for playing in. There is something to see at any time of the year - bulbs, cherry blossom and lilacs in the spring; roses, giant water lilies and bedding plants in the summer; berries and autumn leaves to kick through in October and November; and holly trees, strawberry trees and camellias in the winter.

Should you tire of wandering in the gardens, there are always the glasshouses. The largest and most impressive are the Temperate House, where you can spot tangerines, grapefruits and avocados, and the steamy Palm House, with coconuts, date palms, bananas

and giant bamboo. Both have walkways running high above the floor level so you can look down on the dizzy depths of tangled foliage before descending once again into the undergrowth of exotic scents and heady blooms. In the basement of the Palm House there is a marine display. You have to lift up young children to see inside many of the displays here.

Catering facilities are good in the summer, with a choice of cafes and kiosks selling the usual range of food and drinks. During the winter there is less choice: during the week only the Orangery restaurant is open. On sunny Sundays you may have to queue for up to 15 minutes, and be prepared to share your table (and children's table manners!) with an unsuspecting member of the public. By far the best thing is to bring a picnic and spread it out somewhere that takes your fancy.

A couple of final points, as well as the ban on dogs, you are also not allowed to bring bikes, trikes or radios into the gardens, or play ball games. This may be a blessing to some, but a disappointment to others. Parking in the surrounding streets can prove difficult at busy times.

FACT FILE

Address: Royal Botanic Gardens, Kew, Richmond, Surrey
TW9 3AB

Telephone: 081 940 1171 (answerphone), 081 332 5000

Directions: By car the A205, South Circular to Kew,
turning off and following the signs to Kew Gardens before
you cross Kew Bridge. Trains run from Waterloo, via Clapham
Junction, Putney, and Richmond, to Kew Bridge station
approximately every 30 minutes. There is a 10 minute walk
across Kew Bridge to the Gardens from the station.
Alternatively the District line tube to Kew Gardens - it is then
about a 5 minute walk. During the summer river boats
run from Westminster to Kew Pier (071 930 2062 for information)

Distance from SW London: 10 miles

Travel Time: 30 to 45 minutes

Opening: Open all the year, except Christmas and New
Year's days. 9.30am to 5.30pm in the winter, and to 6.00pm in
the summer (7.00pm Sundays and Bank Holidays).
Glasshouses close at 4.30pm Mondays to Saturdays, and
5.00pm on Sundays

Prices: £4.00 adults, £1.50 5-to-16-year-olds. Under-5's
free. Family ticket (2 adults and up to 4 children £10.00)

Nappy Changing Facilities: Yes (Victoria Gate)

Restaurant Facilities: Yes, 10.00am to 5.00pm

High Chairs: Yes - no straps

Nearby: Kew Bridge Steam Museum, across the river has a
breathtaking array of steam powered machinery, open most
weekends. Take a walk down the river towpath - perhaps
all the way to Richmond Half Tide Lock, an impressive piece
of Victorian engineering - or even as far as Richmond town
centre. Kew itself offers many charming little shops, selling
curios of all sorts

Polesden Lacey

IF YOU LIKE dreaming, try wandering around the gardens at Polesden Lacey, and muse on how life would have been here ninety years ago - elegant ladies with parasols, fine dresses, delicate dishes, and children safely tucked away with governesses. Then come back to earth with a jolt as your delightful offspring hurtle towards a muddy puddle or go puce in the face as you try to cajole them to put their gloves on.

Polesden Lacey is a beautiful Regency house, formally owned by the playwright and politician Sheridan, and overlooking a wonderful secluded valley in the midst of Surrey. The grounds, which are very extensive, are great for walking in with children. There are gravel paths through walled rose arbours, formal gardens with iris and lavender separated by box hedges (great for hide and seek), and rolling lawns and terraces with stunning views of the North Downs. The Long Walk, Nuns' Walk and Admiral's Walks are short trails through the woodland, fields and terraces that make up the estate. None taking more than half an hour to complete, they provide good routes to leisurely stroll around the grounds. Although somewhat muddy in places after wet weather, they are suitable for pushchairs. The estate is full of little nooks and crannies that most children will delight to explore - our children's favourite is the half-timbered thatched bridge with steps up, and the chance to gaze down at the occasional car passing in the lane below. The bridge leads to an orchard of lime and cherry trees - ideal for picnics.

Being owned by the National Trust, Polesden Lacey offers reasonable additional facilities: a restaurant with outside tables situated in a pretty courtyard, a National Trust gift shop (quite a few children's toys and books), toilets with nappy change table. There are plenty of good picnic spots, although not on the main lawns around the house. You may also visit the house -but not with pushchairs.

For a good day out, though, you could have lunch in one of the

many nearby Surrey pubs. We particularly like The White Horse at Shere, which, although not specifically catering for families, allows children in a side bar. It does good meals, and has a lovely mellow atmosphere, with wood panelling, old oak beams and log fires in the winter. Shere village is charming - complete with small streets, antique shops, and ducks cavorting in the stream - its only drawback is the number of people there at weekends! If you fancy walking from Shere as well as at Polesden Lacey, there are several public footpaths from the village too.

FACT FILE

Address: Polesden Lacey, Bookham, Near Dorking, Surrey
RH5 6BD

Telephone: 0372 458203/452048

Directions: Located just off the A246 between
Leatherhead and Guildford. Signposted from Great Bookham

Distance from SW London: 30 miles

Travel Time: 45 minutes

Opening: Grounds are open daily all year 11.00am to 6.00pm
or dusk. The house is open in the afternoons only, and is
restricted to certain days. The restaurant is open from
11.00am Wednesday to Sunday, except in January, February
and March when it is only open at the weekend. It closes
daily from 2.00pm to 2.30pm, reopening for tea until
5.30pm in the summer, and 4.30pm in the winter. Last orders
30 minutes before closing

Prices: Grounds only adults £2.50 in the summer, £2.00 in
the winter. Children under 17 half price, and under-5's free.
House £2.50, or £3.50 Sundays and Bank Holidays

Nappy Changing Facilities: Yes

Restaurant Facilities: Yes

High Chairs: Yes

Nearby: Shere village, with its pretty stream and shops.
Walks on the North Downs, around Box Hill

Windsor Town and Great Park

W INDSOR IS PERFECT for a picnic and a really full day - wonderful for the long days of summer. There is an almost endless choice of nearby picnic spots - Runnymede by the river; the rural tranquility of the Great Park, where you can often catch polo matches in the summer; the fields and pastures around Datchet.

As the Thames meanders gently through lush meadows past Windsor, our favourite spot is actually very close to the centre of Windsor, but over the river in Eton. Cross over Windsor River Bridge to Eton, it is generally quieter than Windsor town there, and walk upstream along the towpath through The Brocas meadow. The broad, open meadow is everything a perfect picnic spot should be: soft, luxuriant grass with buttercups, daisies, clover and dandelions, the river gently lapping the banks, and spectacular views of Windsor Castle and Eton College as a backdrop. Sit on the banks and watch everyone messing about in boats - some vigilance is required here if your children are anything like ours - or pick a patch further back in the meadow, where it is more peaceful and shadier. Or just continue walking along the towpath through woods and pastures. Watch out for bicycles on the towpath though, as the coaches for the Eton College oarsmen pound along the bank shouting encouragement (or abuse) to the crews! (It may be quieter in a few years time when the controversial new rowing course is built upstream at Dorney, but then there won't be so much entertainment. . .)

Alternatively, stay on the Windsor side of the river and walk upstream along the promenade, past fishermen and river boats, towards the Alexandra Gardens. You will see plenty of enthusiastic swans, ducks and geese to feed (if you want to lose your fingers!). About half a mile upstream from the bridge you can picnic in the gardens. There is a small toddler funfair nearby with about five or six rides (£1.00 for four rides). On a really hot day the Alexandra Gardens have the advantage over the Eton side of the river of offering lots of large, shady trees.

In Windsor town there is plenty to see and do. The Castle is the largest castle in England, and you can walk around the grounds free. It is open every day (except Garter Day, the 13th June), but can be subject to closure at short notice (0753 831118 to check). The Changing of the Guard is at 11.00am daily from May to early August, and alternate days the rest of the year. If the weather is poor there are many museums - Queen Mary's Dolls House, the Royalty and Empire exhibition at the Windsor & Eton Central station, or perhaps the Household Cavalry Museum.

If you fancy the sights horse-drawn carriage rides go from the taxi stand outside Windsor castle, but at £19.00 for a half hour trip the cost may be prohibitive. Alternatively try a river boat (£4.20 adults, £2.10 children from one to thirteen years, for a two-hour trip), or an open top bus (0753 855755 for details).

Periodically through the summer Windsor Great Park is the site for international and national polo matches. These would be a day out in themselves. All the glamour of a major sporting event - expensive cars, champagne, strawberries and picnic hampers - but without the crowds that are often so intimidating with young children. Even the busiest events are very accessible. Children are fascinated by the spry polo ponies, and there are usually horsey exhibitions and trade stands.

Park your car in one of the designated car parks (approximately £10.00 per car for an international event) and walk up with your picnic to large, free grassy enclosures alongside the field. Alternatively you can pay a lot more to go into one of the stands to rub shoulders with the cognoscenti... In summer, from around the start of May, polo is on every day except Monday, with matches two or three times a week, and major international events three times a year. All are held in the Guards Polo Club in the centre of the Park. Details from the Polo Club (0784 434212). Tickets can be bought in advance from Ticket Master (071 344 4444).

FACT FILE

Address: Windsor, Berkshire

Telephone: 0753 852010 Windsor Tourist Information Centre

Directions: By car take either the M4 (junction 6) or M3
(junction 3) motorways. Parking in Windsor town can be
difficult - try the station car parks, or along Meadow Lane
on the Eton side of the river (in which case junction 5, the
Eton exit off the M4 and approach Eton through Datchet).
Trains from Waterloo via Clapham Junction, Putney and
Richmond to Windsor & Eton Riverside. Also trains from
Paddington to Slough, and then take local train to Windsor &
Eton Central Station. For the Great Park approach via Egham
(junction 13 off the M25), and Old Windsor

Distance from SW London: 25 miles

Travel Time: 1 hour

Nappy Changing Facilities: No. Toilets in the station car park
in Windsor, and The Brocas car park in Eton

Restaurant Facilities: Choice of pubs and restaurants

High Chairs: Pizzaland has four

Nearby: The Courage Shire Horse Centre on the A4
between Maidenhead and Reading (junction 8/9 of the M4) is
open from the beginning of March to October. Tours and
displays in a working stable with huge Shire horses (0628 824848).

OTHER BOOKS FROM TWO HEADS PUBLISHING

THE BOOKSHOPS OF LONDON
A comprehensive guide to over 500 bookshops in and around
London. The lively and informative listings present the shops by
subject specialisation, in 23 categories from Antiquarian to
Women. A must for every book buyer, browser and book-loving
visitor to London. *Pbk, 208pp, £6.99.*

THE ORGANIC & SUSTAINABLE FARM HOLIDAY GUIDE
This unique guide contains details of organic & sustainable
farms in England, Scotland, Wales, Ireland and France offering
facilities to the holiday-maker and visitor. Enjoy a farm holiday
or bed & breakfast break with a difference, arrange a working
holiday and earn your keep, visit the farms for a day out and
buy wholesome food fresh from the fields. *Pbk, 192pp, £7.99.*

BREATHING SPACES
24 bike rides within easy reach of London. A great mix of on-
and off-road routes, easily accessible by car or train: all day rides
for mountain bikers or tourers, leisurely country lanes, family
rides. With route maps, details of places to see and refreshment
stops. *Pbk, 170pp, £7.99.*

COX'S RURAL RIDES
36 bike rides in the south-east which will take you off the beaten
track and along unspoilt country lanes. The choice of tours
ranges from short excursions to day trips - something for every
cyclist. The illustrated and easy to follow descriptions include
route maps, details of places to see, fascinating local history and
where to stop for food and drink.

*All Two Heads books are available from good bookshops or can be ordered
direct from the publisher. Please send a cheque payable to Two Heads
Publishing to the value of the cover price plus £1 post & packing for the
first copy and 50p for each additional copy.*

Two Heads Publishing, 12A Franklyn Suite, The Priory,
Haywards Heath, West Sussex RH16 3LB.

NOTES

COMMENTS

We would be grateful for your comments on this first edition of *DAYS OUT With Kids*. If you have any suggested recommendations for inclusion in subsequent editions we shall be delighted to hear from you.

Please write to us using the form below, or if you prefer not to tear a page out of your book send us a letter.

From:

Outing:

Comments on this edition:

Comments for next edition:

Please send this form to:

Two Heads Publishing, 12A Franklyn Suite,
The Priory, Haywards Heath, West Sussex,
RH16 3LB

NOTES

The National Childbirth Trust

Alexandra House Oldham Terrace Acton
London W3 6NH Telephone: 081-992 8637

" The National Childbirth Trust offers information and support in pregnancy, childbirth and early parenthood and aims to enable every parent to make informed choices."

The National Childbirth Trust (NCT) is Britain's best-known charity concerned with education for parenthood. It is run by, and for, parents through its network of 350 branches and groups. There are a variety of services to help expectant parents choose the approach to pregnancy, birth and feeding best suited to them and to provide guidance and encouragement to new parents.

The NCT offers help and support to members
and non-members alike.

- ◆ Antenatal classes
- ◆ Breastfeeding counselling
- ◆ Postnatal support
- ◆ Research on maternity issues
- ◆ Education in schools
- ◆ Representation on local health committees

Registered no. 2370573 (England) ● Registered charity no. 801395